Models
— of —
Priestly Formation

PAST, PRESENT, AND FUTURE

MSGR. CHARLES M. MURPHY

A Herder & Herder Book
The Crossroad Publishing Company
New York

For the faculty and students
of the North American College
with gratitude

The Crossroad Publishing Company
16 Penn Plaza – 481 Eighth Avenue, Suite 1550
New York, NY 10001

Printed in the United States of America

The text of this book is set in 11/15 Goudy Old Style.
The display face is Calligraphic 421.

Library of Congress Cataloging-in-Publication Data

Murphy, Charles M.
    Models of priestly formation : past, present, future / Charles M. Murphy.
      p. cm. – (A Herder & Herder Book)
    Includes bibliographical references.
    ISBN-13: 978-0-8245-2402-9 (alk. paper)
    ISBN-10: 0-8245-2402-0 (alk. paper)
    1. Catholic Church – Clergy – Training of. 2. Catholic theological
seminaries. 3. Priesthood – Catholic Church. I. Title.   II. Series.
BX903.M87 2006
230.07′32 – dc22
                                        2006016423

1 2 3 4 5 6 7 8 9 10   12 11 10 09 08 07 06

Contents

Introduction

The Present Moment in Priestly Formation

"These are difficult days for seminaries." This was a comment made to me in a conversation with Ronald Witherup, S.S., provincial superior of the Sulpician Fathers, a pioneering religious organization in seminary education.

The difficulties actually are many. They concern not merely the decline in seminary candidates in many parts of the world. They refer not only to the fewer and fewer members of the religious organizations like the Sulpicians who staff seminaries. The most important question is even more fundamental: What is a seminary and what kind of formation should the seminary provide today for candidates to the priesthood?

One after another papal visitations of seminaries in the United States have expressed this concern. The latest, which took place in the fall of 2005, was given the specific charge of investigating the adequacy of training the seminaries are providing for living a celibate life. Earlier visitations were prompted by such issues as mixing priesthood and lay ministry candidates in the same classrooms, fidelity to the official teaching of the church, the respective roles of spiritual and human formation, the necessity and extent of pastoral experiences during the years of formation, as well as the quality of philosophical and theological studies.

I was part of a papal visitation team during the study mandated by Pope John Paul II between 1983 and 1985. All the visits followed the same format. The team was headed by a bishop, and the actual visitation was compressed into a single week. In advance the team was given extensive documentation provided by the seminary to be visited. Following the visit a report was made both to the national conference of bishops and the Vatican's Congregation for Catholic Education. A report eventually was given as well to the seminary itself. In this visitation and the others it was only the current model of seminary formation that provided the context for the recommendations: no new or different models were considered.

This is what is now changing. In the current crises of scandalous behavior in the priesthood and the phenomenon of departures from the priesthood especially in the early years after ordination, something new is taking place. Different forms of seminary are emerging and some have been around long enough for their future promise to be evaluated.

This book aims to recapitulate the history of the modern development of seminaries, the spiritual impetus from which they originated, their varying conceptions of the priesthood, their overall strengths and weaknesses. In light of this history we will examine new models of seminary formation that are beginning to emerge. In conclusion we will outline what a more adequate seminary formation might look like to meet the pastoral needs of the church at this moment in her history.

The Present Moment in the Church

Seminary formation is conditioned and shaped by prevailing historical circumstances. The seminaries of the formative post-Reformation period in Roman Catholicism sought to reestablish clerical discipline and to elevate the general competency of parish priests. Later, in France, out of a powerful spiritual matrix called "the French School," a new type of seminary formation was created, aimed at transforming the priesthood from a mere social institution to a spiritual force. With the Second Vatican Council and its aftermath, the seminary was seen to need adaptation so that the church could make a more vital pastoral connection with the world.

After the optimism of those early post-conciliar years when the church was at its institutional apex following World War II, we are now experiencing the full effects of secularizing trends in a more affluent society. Parish life in Europe is in great disarray, and in the United States regular participation by the faithful in weekly worship has declined among Catholics to levels below that of Protestants. As society no longer reinforces religious values and practices, catechetical efforts by the church appear feeble and inadequate. A "new evangelization" is being promoted, "new" in the sense that even traditional Catholics need to be convinced again of the value of religious faith in their lives.

It is not surprising that in these new, changing circumstances, new models of seminary formation are emerging. These new models have the general characteristic of creating close-knit Christian communities in which persons who are being called to the priesthood can develop their vocations. These communities before and after ordination provide the support, challenge, and accountability required for priests to flourish in their vocation.

What I Have Learned as a Seminary Rector

As I was writing this book I reflected back on my years as rector of the North American College in Rome. The college is made up of three departments: a seminary residence for candidates studying at Roman universities who will be serving as priests in the United

States; a continuing education–sabbatical program for priests who have served a number of years; and a residence for priests pursuing graduate degrees. What had those years taught me?

A major theme of this book is personal conversion to the Gospel way of life as a central element of formation. How can a seminary formation program provide the conditions for such a transformation that is after all a work of the Holy Spirit? I have come to the following conclusions.

Fidelity to prayer, especially the form known as *lectio divina* ("divine reading"), converts. The heart and soul personally addressed by God through daily reflection upon the scriptures are changed. The priority of prayer in the seminary, both liturgical and private, must be maintained despite all distractions.

Living for an extended period in a foreign country converts. The purification and spiritual liberty that come from the loss of personal props such as frequent home visits, owning your own automobile, and access to your favorite pastimes and entertainments contribute greatly to conversion to the Gospel. It helps the candidate clarify what he needs for a happy life and identify "the one thing necessary."

Theological study converts. The spiritual direction relationship influences very directly growth in the interiorization of the Gospel way of life. But even in spiritual direction a subjective element is present that the objective norm of success in theological study diminishes. Laziness can invade a life separated from the world, while theological study requires active engagement. Homilies delivered by seminarians are for a rector an accurate reflection of whether they have made a connection between their childhood faith and new theological insights.

Working with and for the poor converts. Seminarians who spent a summer, for example, living in Calcutta at a home for the dying sponsored by the Missionaries of Charity returned different. They were less inclined to adopt the "institutional mentality" of complaint about the quality of life and services the seminary provides them.

Being immersed in the diocese of Rome converts. The pope, pastor of the universal church, is also bishop of the diocese of Rome. Seminarians who are privileged to have frequent contact with the Holy Father at his audiences and liturgies adopt almost unconsciously a new pastoral vision and love and loyalty to him.

The seminary community itself should convert, but here the North American College labors under some disadvantages. The formative power of being a member on a daily basis of a community of persons whose entire focus is upon prayer, study, and vocational discernment is somewhat diminished if there is a constant stream of visitors and external demands. As someone with a monastic background who lived at the college once commented, it is like living in Stazione Termini, the principal rail station of Rome! As rector I felt the obligation constantly to bring the community back to its true priorities.

I would offer one other comment about seminaries and conversion. Quite often we admitted candidates who in adulthood had undergone a conversion, sometimes dramatic, to Christ. In the emotional power of that event they sometimes confused a calling to become a Christian with a vocation to the priesthood. The formation faculty who more and more are engaged with older candidates need the skill to help these candidates with a deeper reflection.

Several persons were of assistance as I wrote this book. Among them I mention Father John O'Malley, S.J., of Weston School of Theology, Cambridge, Massachusetts, who spent time discussing my project with me and giving guidance in the area in which he has great expertise, the creation of the seminary by the Council of Trent; Father Anthony Figueiredo, who accompanied me on my visit to Redemptoris Mater Seminary, Kearny, New Jersey; and Bishop Eric Aumonier, bishop of Versailles, first superior of La Maison Saint-Augustin in Paris. In addition, I appreciate greatly the careful review of the manuscript by Cardinal Avery Dulles, S.J., and his encouragement.

One

The Creation
of the Seminary

The pastoral commission entrusted to every priest is to be esteemed as so elevated as to be on the level of the divine, especially because of the power to celebrate the sacrament of the Eucharist. It is superior even to the offices of the angels themselves. Who then could deny that even more grand, and, for that reason more desirable, is the dignity of the bishop who has the authority to confer upon others the power and worthiness to celebrate this sacrament? As for myself, I prepare to exercise this episcopal office full of admiration, and even astonishment.

— ST. CHARLES BORROMEO[1]

The sixteenth century was a pivotal moment in the Catholic Church. It saw not only the rise of Protestantism but also the transition of the church from the Middle Ages to the modern era. In that century the Council of Trent was summoned to respond to these challenges. Its decrees shaped Catholicism for centuries, right up to the Second Vatican Council.

One of the most influential and enduring achievements of that council was the creation of the seminary. The seminary was to reform the clergy to reform the church. In many significant ways it succeeded. In this chapter we will examine Trent's decrees calling for the establishment of a seminary in every diocese. We will propose St. Charles Borromeo as an exemplary model of what was happening in that period, outline the spiritual impulses that inspired these reforms, and, finally, give a first assessment of the strengths and limitations of the Tridentine seminary.

Much has been written about the disarray in parishes and dioceses and their clergy that was then occurring. The Council of Trent aimed its reforms directly at this aspect of the church's life and activity. But the life of the Catholic Church then as now is much broader and richer. The religious orders in many places carried much of the pastoral burden through their preaching missions and educational institutions. Lay-led confraternities are another example of how a vigorous religious life took place outside parish structures. Members of various professions, businesses, and crafts formed themselves into religious organizations that maintained their own churches and conducted numerous works of charity. Michelangelo, for example, belonged to one such society whose primary voluntary service was the proper burial of the indigent poor. Trent had nothing to say about this important dimension of the church's reality.

Soon after his election as pope on December 26, 1559, Gianangelo Medici, Pope Pius IV, decided to reconvene the Council of Trent that Pope Paul III had called in 1545. Under Paul, the council conducted two sessions, 1545–47 and 1550–55. The council after much confusion was helped in finding its focus by Cardinal Giovanni Maria del Monte, bishop of Palestrina and papal legate. Speaking on February 8, 1547, he declared: "Why all these jeremiads about the abuses in the church, of which we are all acquainted? Why wrangle about the question of power? This aim of our reforms is the revival of pastoral ministry, the care of souls." The care of souls, *cura animarum*, became the council's driving force. As Hubert Jedin, the council's historian, comments, "This was the first time that this purpose was clearly stated in a plenary assembly of the council."[2]

It was therefore through a better care of souls that the Council of Trent sought to bring about the reform of the church. It was a moral reform, a return to Christian discipline of life among the faithful, and their models and leaders were to be the newly disciplined clergy. The council did not concern itself therefore with dramatic changes in church structures and organization that the Protestant reformers were calling for. In the council's view, since these were of divine institution, they could not be altered.

Paul IV Caraffa (1555–59), Paul III's successor, was not convinced that an ecumenical council was the best vehicle for facing the Protestant threat. Beautiful conciliar documents are not the way to root out heresy. Paul IV, that "old fighter," as he was called,[3] severe and intolerant, believed more in the Inquisition and the Index of Forbidden Books. He also had other preoccupations, such as driving out of Italy the influence of the kingdom of Spain. His programs did have some limited effect. In February 1556, for example, 113 bishops who were living at the papal court were sent back home to care for their neglected dioceses.

In turning to Pius IV Medici (1559–65) as Paul IV's successor, the cardinals were seeking someone more moderate and genial who was at the same time committed to reform. Pius IV reconvened the Council of Trent for its final, crucial phase (1562–63). Cardinal Giovanni Morone, who had been confined by Paul IV on suspicion of heresy, was called to lead this final session, which produced the decrees for the reform of the clergy. Cardinal Reginald Pole of England, who also had been under suspicion, drew on his experience in the training of priests to help give shape to the institution of the seminary.

Trent's Call for Seminaries to Train Priests

What the Council of Trent called for regarding the training of candidates for the priesthood was limited to making provision for poor boys with no resources of their own to become priests. Beyond these seminaries no further education was required before these candidates became ordained. Other routes to the priesthood were possible for persons of a different social class and more means.

A good example of someone who had no need for such a seminary was the nephew of the prince-bishop of the diocese of Trent itself, Gian Lodovico Madruzzo, who eventually succeeded his uncle as bishop. In 1561 the painter Giovanni Battista Maroni was commissioned to produce an impressive wall-length portrait of the nephew. He is portrayed at about the age of twenty. He is elegantly attired in black ecclesiastical robes, a cassock surmounted by a satin soprano. In his right hand he holds a pair of tan leather gloves. His favorite hound is at his side. His noble head is subtly molded, his eyes fixed upon the viewer with an intent, intelligent gaze. A young man of this stature would have been totally out of place in the Tridentine seminary. It was only in the late nineteenth and early twentieth centuries that attendance in a seminary would be required, and even then there were exceptions like Pope Pius XII, who as a member of the Roman nobility was tutored at home.

Even so, the Tridentine seminary was a considerable advance beyond the apprentice system, which was the ordinary path to the priesthood for many. A young man simply apprenticed himself to a priest as someone would to a blacksmith and learned priestcraft by observation. This is how the long-prevailing "ritual Mass" came about. A person of such limited education, in order not to disgrace himself and the congregation in celebrating the liturgy, had to be given precise regulations about the right thumb being placed over the left in the gesture of prayer and the right foot and not the left being used to mount the first of the altar steps. Penitential books (*libri poenitentiales*) told the priest-confessor in precise terms what penances to impose for which particular sins. No homily of any consequence was expected at Mass, this task being left to the better-educated religious orders.

On July 15, 1563, during the twenty-third session of the Council of Trent, the following decree was issued.

> The age of adolescence, unless it is properly guided, is given to the pursuit of worldly pleasures. Unless from their most impressionable years youth are shaped toward religious piety before the habits of vice invade, never perfectly and without the greatest and singular help of our omnipotent God would they persevere in the discipline of the church. This synod therefore decrees that a certain number of the youth of its city be nourished and religiously educated in the disciplines of the church.[4]

The idea of a "seminary" (literally "seed bed") organized around the bishop was not a new notion. It goes back to St. Augustine (354–430), the bishop of Hippo, whose desire was to live the celibate life in a community of priests and candidates for the priesthood. The faithful of his diocese were proud of the simplicity of life practiced by their bishop and priests; for them it mirrored the first Christian communities described in the Acts of the Apostles, who were said to hold all things in common (Acts 4:32). According to Augustine's biographer Peter Brown, "Augustine had made the acceptance of this life a condition of serving him as a member of the clergy. Anyone who defaulted from this agreement would be deprived of holy orders."[5]

In later centuries cathedral chapters established schools for the education of poor boys. The priests of the chapter comprised the faculty and taught various subjects. The students performed various chores around the cathedral, moving the chairs and helping with the ceremonies. What Trent was doing therefore in requiring every diocese to establish its own seminary was very much in keeping with this long-established tradition. According to James A. O'Donohoe, "The seminary legislation of Trent was fundamentally a return to the ancient practice of grouping candidates around their bishop and having them formed morally and intellectually under his supervision."[6]

The curriculum of the seminaries was set forth by the council in broad terms. Students were to be exposed to literature and the humanities; they were to learn the basics of ecclesiastical chant and the rubrics for conducting ceremonies. They should learn something about Sacred Scripture in order to preach as well as elements of doctrine and morality for their pastoral applications.

The Rule of Life for the seminary included attendance at daily Mass and the opportunity for private confession at least once a month. At the beginning of their entrance into seminary, the seminarians were to receive tonsure and begin to wear clerical attire as part of their separation from the world.

St. Charles Borromeo and the First Tridentine Seminaries: A Case Study

St. Charles Borromeo (1538–84) moved to establish the first seminaries as decreed by Trent within months of the council's conclusion in his own diocese of Milan. He served that diocese as archbishop while at the same time residing in Rome as the papal secretary of state for his uncle, Pope Pius IV. The pope had named his young nephew as head of the commission to resume the council. Although Charles never traveled to Trent, he followed the deliberations very closely. It was said of him, "Charles throughout his life would be for the council, against the pre-conciliar and the anti-conciliar."[7]

Nicolò Ormaneto, vicar general of Milan, was appointed to create the foundations for the seminaries. He was well suited for the task, having spent time in England working with Cardinal Pole for the restoration of Catholicism. Part of that program was a return to the ancient tradition of the cathedral grammar school. Cardinal Pole, even before Trent, required a period of several weeks' duration for the training of candidates for the priesthood.

The new seminaries recruited adolescents. Some were set up in urban centers, others in Bergamo, Como, and Novara. In addition to these, other institutions were established for the retraining of priests already ordained and for older candidates. By 1580 Charles had obtained authority for a degree-granting institution that brighter candidates could attend.

Charles initially looked to the new Society of Jesus to help him staff his seminaries. He was careful to obtain a papal directive that no seminarian could be recruited from his institutions to become a Jesuit. The life of the seminary and its routines reflected Charles's absorption of the spirituality of St. Ignatius Loyola, founder of the Jesuits. Regular retreats based upon the *Spiritual Exercises* of St. Ignatius were integrated into the seminary year. Other Ignatian features were incorporated into the practice of mental prayer, regular examination of conscience, personal mortification, and spiritual direction. From Charles himself came the emphasis upon the Eucharist as the Real Presence of Christ to be adored and reverenced as well as limited engagement in pastoral activity.

Preaching took a central place in the curriculum of the seminary. Trent coined the phrase that preaching was to be the *principium munus* (the "primary task") of bishops and priests. In this way the bishops were aiming at taking control of the preaching in their dioceses that in large part had been given over to religious orders. The preaching was to be of a specific type — not erudite or particularly scholarly but pastoral. According to the Institutions of the first provincial council of Milan in 1565, preachers had two functions: to acquaint the people with Sacred Scripture, the articles of the creed, the prayers of the Mass, the sacraments of the church, and the Ten Commandments; and, second, to explain the way of life that leads to salvation including the virtues to be cultivated, the vices to be avoided, and the rewards and punishments appropriate for each. According to Benjamin Westervelt, "Harping upon sin was the staple of the Caroline ideal of pastoral preaching."[8] Federico Borromeo, Charles's cousin and later his successor as archbishop, summarized well what it meant, according to Charles, to be an effective preacher. "The humblest pastor," he said, "can fulfill his obligation [to preach] if he knows his flock, clings to the Scriptures, and diligently practices his preaching ministry."[9]

Always a man of detail, Charles, once he took up residence in Milan after much pleading with the pope, kept a careful eye on the seminarians. He wanted to see lists provided by the faculty of the best potential preachers. They would be given extra duties beyond the usual parish assignments, conducting preaching missions throughout the archdiocese. Charles felt obliged to provide the example of being a devoted preacher. By nature he was not a gifted speaker. He spoke with a speech impediment but with great sincerity. That quality, in addition to the witness of his own life, made him convincing.

The vision shaping Charles's conception of the seminary was the salvation of souls. Future priests were to heed the admonition of St. Paul to Timothy to "make yourself an example to believers in speech and behavior, in love, fidelity, and purity" (1 Tim. 4:12). Thus, in the ideal seminarian, "prayer, renunciation of self, and penitential asceticism were not particular individual exercises but energies placed at the service of the pastoral ministry."[10] The priest thus formed would be a "luminous example to the faithful."[11] According to Charles, the primary duties of the priest were to be present to his people in the parish, chant the psalms to God on their behalf, to pray, to study, and to preach. "Tutto il resto non e di loro pertinenza" ("Everything else does not pertain to them").[12]

Charles Borromeo died during the night of November 2, 1584, at the age of forty-six, his frail body worn out by the extreme penances he practiced. As a pastoral bishop he had mixed success. The clergy did not like him and were never fully won over to his reforms. His consuming passion to elevate the quality of preaching in the parishes met with only limited success. What secured his reputation among the people was the personal charity he demonstrated when Milan was devastated by the plague. He personally ministered to the sick and even went so far as ordering the velvet draperies of his episcopal palace to be cut up and made into pantaloons for the poor. People could tell which room of the palace their garment came from by the color. And, of course, among his lasting legacies was the launching of the Tridentine seminary, giving it a shape and vision that would influence the church for centuries to come.

The Priestly Spirituality of St. Charles Borromeo and Its Continuing Influence

When on that June day in 1577 Charles delivered the ordination homily cited at the beginning of this chapter, he was expressing a very elevated conception of the dignity of the priesthood and episcopate, claiming it exceeded even that of the angels. He did not always hold this view. During his early years as a cardinal in the curia he felt no need to pursue holy orders. In Rome he enjoyed the life of a Renaissance prince, hosting humanistic seminars and the company of distinguished artists and scholars.

Charles's personal conversion seems to have been prompted by the sudden premature death of his older brother Federico in November of 1562. In such a circumstance he might have been expected to set aside all ideas of being ordained and to take up familial duties in place of his deceased brother. Instead he was inspired to embrace the ascetical life for which he is renowned and to seek holy orders. The contemplation of one's own death and the transitoriness of all things are prominent features of post-Tridentine spirituality. Everybody seemed to be preoccupied with his or her personal salvation and the possibility of eternal damnation. The necessity for conversion from sin was a major theme of the preaching of the era. The prayerful contemplation of Christ's passion was a central element in this piety. By pondering the extreme sufferings that Christ underwent for our sake, the human soul could become convinced of the enormity of human sinfulness and of the divine love that redeemed it.

The sacraments of penance and the Holy Eucharist assumed ever greater import in post-Tridentine spirituality. It is hard to imagine a post-Tridentine priest apart from his roles at the altar and in the confessional. The power to celebrate Mass for the people and bring about the miracle of transubstantiation of the bread and wine into the real presence of Christ and the power to forgive sins were the true foundation for the high esteem given to the priest. Human nature, frail and flawed, needed the saving remedy of divine grace communicated in the sacraments of penance and Holy Eucharist. These two, as Charles and his age conceived them, were divine medicines for the soul in its sinful condition.[13]

The Eucharist, the sacramental presence of the Lord, was to be approached therefore with the greatest awe and reverence. One of Charles's major concerns was the dignified celebration of the liturgy and the proper care of sacred spaces, especially for the reservation of the Eucharist. The faithful often were reluctant to enter churches that came to be associated with moldering tombs. Charles paid much attention to church architecture, and one of the most prominent features of the sanctuaries he designed was the spectacular tabernacles that dominated sacred space, dwarfing even the altar of sacrifice. The signs we still see in Italian sacristies commanding *silenzio* owe their origin to Charles. Reception of the sacrament of penance was to be frequent, for penance was the best preparation for the worthy reception of the Eucharist. Charles himself confessed every day.

A justly famous representation of this spirituality may be found in the paintings of Caravaggio (1571–1610). His style of painting, called *verismo*, was encouraged by the decrees of Trent. Subjects were to be portrayed in their ordinary human life without the idealization found in the heroic figures of Renaissance art. They were to exemplify moral goodness and inspire viewers to a conversion of life. Such works of art were needed to popularize Trent's program of reform, and Caravaggio is an outstanding exemplar.

In Caravaggio's stunning painting of the recognition scene of the Risen Christ in the breaking of the bread at Emmaus, for example, Christ is seen as an ordinary young man, beardless and with luxuriant hair. The action of Christ and the startled reaction of the disciples are projected forward into the viewer's space to engage the heart and inspire devotion. The dramatic use of light, a symbol of divine grace, floods the scene and highlights each object. Art critics have criticized Caravaggio for his placement of apples, grapes, figs, and pomegranates upon the table at an event taking place in the spring, but these also serve a didactic purpose. Their bruised and spotted appearance demonstrates the transitoriness of all earthly things.[14]

According to Trent, the leaders and models in Christian conversion for the whole Christian people were priests. As St. Ignatius Loyola had taught in his *Spiritual Exercises,* there are two banners to follow, the banner of Christ and the banner of Satan, and everyone must make a choice. The church militant on earth has to do battle with the forces of evil, and so it needs a disciplined corps of soldier-priests in its army to lead the people into combat. The seminary was the training ground, the boot camp for these leaders.

This is the spirituality of the priesthood that inspired the Tridentine seminary. Its continuing vitality can be seen in a work on the diocesan priesthood written in the nineteenth century, *The Eternal Priesthood* by Cardinal Henry Edward Manning (1808–92). In Manning's characterization, this spirituality represents a "virile simplicity" (*simplicitas virilis*). This phrase has resonances of nineteenth-century boarding schools such as Eton and Harrow, but it is an accurate description of the aim of the Tridentine seminary. This is how Manning summarizes this training and the role of the bishop:

> The episcopate has been defined as the order that has spiritual power to rule and to propagate the church of God by the perpetuity of sacred ordination. The chief office, therefore, of the bishop is to choose out, to try, to train, and so to make perfect, the youths who are to be admitted to the priesthood. From twelve years old, as the Council of Trent orders, they should be trained in the seminary, already admitted to the clerical state by tonsure. From twelve to twenty-four they are under the eye and hand of the bishop, for though others work under him, he is so the head and source of

their training that the Council of Trent calls the seminary *episcopalis praesentia.*[15]

As part of his program to reform the diocesan clergy, Charles had founded the Oblates of St. Anselm (later renamed the Oblates of St. Anselm and St. Charles). This quasi-religious congregation was modeled after the Oratorians of St. Philip Neri. These diocesan priests continued through their association to receive seminary formation even into the actual practice of ministry in parishes. The perennial need for such an association may be inferred by a lament of Cardinal Manning about the priests of his day. He says, "Priests dwelling alone are in an abnormal, unecclesiastical, unsacerdotal state, which often has grave dangers and is never free from many disadvantages."[16]

When in the twentieth century Blessed John XXIII convoked a new reforming council, the Second Vatican Council, the achievements of the Council of Trent provided a model and inspiration. As a young priest, Angelo Roncalli had written his doctoral dissertation on the pastoral visits of Charles as archbishop of Milan to the seminary founded in Bergamo. Pope John's startling decision to convoke another ecumenical council might have been predicted by the very date he chose for his inauguration as pope, November 4, the memorial of St. Charles Borromeo.

First Assessment

Charles's intention in establishing institutions specifically designed for the training of priests was to equip diocesan priests with the moral respectability and competence associated with the members of religious orders. For this reason this model of seminary was later criticized because, it was alleged, it was more suited to produce monks than parish priests. A more accurate comparison, however, on this type of seminary is not the monastic novitiate but military training institutions.

To draw out this comparison, a recent study by David Lipsky of the United States Military Academy at West Point is enlightening. I list four dimensions of life at West Point that parallel the seminary of St. Charles.

First, West Point, like the seminary, emphasizes *separation from the world and its values.* In the study, a faculty member at the academy is quoted as saying something a seminary leader might also have said: "There's a growing difference between the values of the military and society, and there always will be."[17]

In language that is almost Pauline, a cadet states:

Before I came here I was totally my own man. My parents respected me. I was in my own car, doing my own thing. Came in here with my bag of underwear. I lost everything. I became an absolute nobody. That's the whole philosophy of West Point — you're literally a bag of underwear. Everything you had before, you're pretty much walking away from it.[18]

Reception Day at West Point can be traumatic. A cadet relates, "You surrender your old self in stages. You've already left behind family and control over your environment."[19] The cadets are given a new set of identical clothing; they take an oath, and then the army cuts off their hair.

Second, *West Point is a trade school to produce soldiers, its single aim.* The seminary also has just one aim, to produce priests. Entrants are to undergo the transformation from being students to becoming soldiers. This is the aura of the academy, that it has a special mission, to make civilians "soldierized." It is that rare place where individuals tackle life's basic questions, like, "Can I do this?" "What kind of person am I?" Cadets arriving at West Point are given a ready-made identity. They are to become "professionals," knowing that a member of a profession commands respect. For many the army is more than a profession; as one recruit put it, "I never thought they should call it a profession. It's more like a calling."[20]

Third, *West Point aims to develop a character of a particular type,* as does the seminary. The developmental model at the Point is "crawl, walk, run" and "be, know, do." Each cadet begins by subscribing to a code of honor: "A cadet will not lie, cheat, or steal or tolerate those who do." Cadets quickly learn that being part of the army means meeting standards that are clear and non-negotiable, that there are benchmarks of expectation and of performance. They are given a sense of honor and accountability. They learn to be part of a motivated chain of command.

Every cadet is evaluated in academic performance, military skills, and physical fitness. The cadet undergoes a total immersion in a twenty-four hour, seven-day environment. No summer vacations are allowed. The military uniform is to be worn at all times. Lipsky comments, "Daily life at West Point is organized the way people in the Middle Ages believed God oversaw the universe; every encounter is supposed to develop the cadets in some way."[21]

Fourth, *entrance requirements are strict.* The principal requirement is that recruits fervently wish to devote their lives to service. The notion of service is key to the meaning of West Point, doing your duty and serving your country. The ideal is that the original commitment to five years of being a soldier after graduation will be extended to a full twenty-year military career. The seminary as well picks persons who feel a call to lifelong service.

The result of this process of forming soldiers is the conviction that you are part of an elite, that you are a superior human being. The indefinable spirit of West Point is expressed in the commonly used word "Huah." The spirit and practice of "Huah" make you feel part of something big and good, that what you have been trained to do has an urgency about it. An institution permeated with such a spirit has a perceptible authenticity about it; its members all give their best effort, look out for each other, and are not driven by monetary gain. Everyone dresses the same and has a clear assignment; the net effect, according to one who observed the life at close range, is feeling blessed.[22]

Lipsky calls West Point an "irony-free zone," a place where sarcasm is out. Everyone is incredibly fit, mentally, physically, and psychologically. People are happy and proud of who they are. The leaders of the academy, as Charles wished the ordained clergy to be, are admired.

Such a portrait may seem excessively positive and the author of this study himself balances it with some criticisms. More and more West Point is beginning to resemble an Ivy League college and departing from its trade school image. Today's graduates often see West Point as a good career move and use that credential to seek other opportunities that are more lucrative. There are, too, aspects of West Point that no seminary would want to emulate, especially preparing people to do violence in combat. The discipline in a seminary pales in comparison with West Point. But in many ways the model of a military school provides an enlightening contemporary example of what a seminary in the time of Charles was supposed to be like.

Life at the academy, like life in a seminary, may seem a throwback to the past, and it is sometimes a cause of wonderment that young people today would be motivated to embrace it. Perhaps part of its attraction lies in its clear difference from the modern world and its ideals of self-fulfillment.

Two

The Seminary in France

A Milieu for Spiritual and Pastoral Formation

Good priests are those who in their ordinary life are models to their flock. They must embody everything the church regards as pure and holy if they are to be perfect priests. They offer up and annihilate their own will, for only by the emptying of self will the Spirit of Jesus Christ come.

— CARDINAL PIERRE DE BÉRULLE[23]

The originators of the new form of priestly formation in France in the sixteenth and seventeenth centuries were a remarkable group of clergy and women religious. Together they comprised a powerful spiritual matrix called "the French School." Their spirituality was the shaping influence of all seminary education down to the Second Vatican Council. In fact, Roman Catholic spirituality and the French School became virtually the same.

In some ways the French School was a reaction against the dry, academic theology called "Scholasticism." It was as well the expression of that realm in religion always suspect by the orthodox — spiritual experience. The founder of the French School, Cardinal Pierre de Bérulle (1575–1629) crystallized their view: "Some distinguish between a mystical and a practical theology, but this is a distinction which I do not wish to employ."[24]

Jean-Jacques Olier (1608–57), founder of the Society of Saint-Sulpice for the training of priests, brought to this spirituality an even greater intensity. His mysticism, sometimes bordering on the strange, helped to popularize Bérulle's thought. Bérulle grounded Christian spirituality upon the great mystery of the Incarnation of God in the person of Jesus Christ. For Olier, in the Incarnation Christ's humanity is not so much united with his divinity as annihilated by it. According to Olier, the Christian, and the priest most of all, must disown the "flesh" and live entirely on the plane of the spirit. In these directions Olier's thought verged on Jansenism, an extreme form of Catholicism with similarities to Calvinistic Puritanism. Human nature for Olier was nothing more than a spiritual obstacle to be transcended. For him, even food and drink were kept to the absolute minimum to sustain life.

St. Vincent de Paul (1580–1660), founder of the Congregation of the Mission, and St. John Eudes (1606–80), founder of the Eudist Fathers, also propagated Bérulle's ideas. Together with the Society of Saint-Sulpice, they joined in a valiant enterprise: to elevate the sad state of the French clergy. St. Vincent, who in his early years as a priest was so scandalized by the condition of the clergy that he considered leaving the priesthood, is quoted as saying, "The church has no worse enemies than her priests."[25]

According to Cardinal Bérulle, the goal of the spiritual life is the reproduction in the individual Christian of the image of Christ. The priest is to be the human sacrament of the divine and heavenly priest, Jesus Christ, to whom his whole life and person are to be configured. Bérulle brought to France the new religious society of diocesan priests founded by St. Philip Neri (1515–95), though in a somewhat different form. But the aim of Bérulle was the same as that of St. Philip — the renewal of the diocesan priesthood.

In this chapter we will explore the inspiring vision of the priest-hood of Bérulle as it came to be exemplified in the Oratory, which he founded, and then see how Olier expanded and popularized these ideas with the establishment of the seminaries of St. Sulpice. We will then summarize the principal themes of this spiritual-ity and give them a first assessment in terms of their continuing impact upon seminary formation.

The "Faith, Fire, and Iron" of St. Philip and the "Authority, Holiness, and Doctrine" of Cardinal Bérulle

It is an amazing example of the religious ferment taking place in France that by 1631 there were seventy-one houses of the Oratory. In 1601, within two years of his ordination, Pierre de Bérulle felt commissioned by God to establish a new foundation composed of diocesan priests. As he articulated it,

> The same God who has reestablished in our days in many religious families the spirit and fervor of their first institution seems to wish also to impart the same grace and favor to the state of the priesthood which is the first, the most essen-tial and necessary office for the church, and to renew in it the state of perfection which fits it according to its ancient practice and first institution.[26]

Calling the diocesan priesthood the "Order of Christ," Bérulle assumed the natural superiority of this order to all the religious orders whose founders were merely human. His goal was to reunite in these priests three perfections, which by his time had become separated: authority, holiness, and doctrine. Personal authority seemed to be the exclusive prerogative of the prelate, holiness the expectation only of the religious, and doctrine the province of academics. Each religious order seemed, in the intention of its founder, to be called to exemplify a particular virtue among the Christian people. The Franciscans modeled poverty, the Carthusians, solitude, the Jesuits, obedience. The singular virtue of the priests of the Oratory must be love of Jesus Christ the eternal high priest, and their most important duty was to pray for the people entrusted to their care. Where priests were once considered merely the menial servants of the rich and powerful, it was impressive and gratifying, once the Oratories were flourishing, to see priests everywhere wearing the cassock as a symbol of their new status.

The Council of Trent began its sessions six years before St. Philip, founder of the Oratory in Rome, was ordained. He had spent many years as a layman, and once ordained he really did not have any employment. Knowing that his temperament was not suited to the structured life of a religious order, he began an informal ministry of hearing confessions and organizing gatherings in his apartment. From these spiritual direction sessions emerged what became known as the "Oratory," a new kind of institution but one that was well suited for the reform of clerical life that the Council of Trent was calling for.

The informal discussions that Philip led as his means of catechizing gradually took on a structure that he called *ragionamento* ("reasoning"). Some text, scriptural or other, was read by a participant. Then all were invited to speak about its meaning from their hearts. Then they were expected to perform some apostolic action, such as caring for the sick or begging alms for the poor. From this developed the triad that Philip called "the fire, the faith, and the iron." The fire is the zealous heart of the believer. The faith is the conviction that the One who gave the Spirit in biblical times is giving it still today. The iron refers to the firm adherence required to the Christian way of life. St. Philip was known to be lighthearted and compassionate, but he was firm in the direction he gave his followers.[27] By design there were few formal rules for the common life of the Oratory. "The chief rule," it was rightly said, "was spiritual direction through Philip, through Philip's example. Instead of vows there were only the virtues of poverty, chastity, and obedience, which were nonetheless lived as though they had been solemnly vowed."[28]

In the form of the Oratory introduced to France by Bérulle, priest members were required to renounce all secular ambitions and religious benefices. With regard to other clergy their houses were to have the same function as the ancient monasteries had for the Christian laity, that is, model communities where all the virtues were practiced: poverty of life, humility, charity, zeal, piety. Very soon, under the second superior general, Père de Condren, the French Oratory shifted focus away from seminary training to undertake other priestly works. One of Condren's dying wishes was that Jean-Jacques Olier, one of his spiritual directees, would undertake the great work of carrying on seminary education.

When Bérulle died on October 2, 1629, he was celebrating Mass facing a representation of the Annunciation of the archangel Gabriel to the Blessed Virgin Mary, a depiction of the stupendous mystery of the Incarnation of the Son of God around which Bérulle had concentrated his whole life and spirituality. Through his inspiration the seminary, which under St. Charles Borromeo had been a place for the reform of morals, became something else: a milieu, separated from the world, for spiritual formation and education. It was said that while Charles relied upon surveillance and a certain suspicion of human behavior as part of the seminary regime, Bérulle and the French School sought to develop interiority of conscience and friendly relations between faculty and students as the principal formative elements for future priests.

Jean-Jacques Olier and the Society of Saint-Sulpice

Among the pioneers in the spiritual development of priests and seminarians was St. Vincent de Paul. His Tuesday days of recollection at the Rue Saint-Lazare for those already ordained and his three-week retreats offered for candidates preparing for ordination, influenced many. Among them was Jean-Jacques Olier. He attended Vincentian retreats and for a period of five years participated in Vincent's program to evangelize rural populations through the organization of parish missions.

That experience taught him many things, among them that the people were in desperate need of the services of good priests. It was only after a prolonged period of two years of spiritual desolation between 1639 and 1641 that it was revealed to him by God that he should undertake the task of training priests. This time of depression, during which Olier felt rejected by God, no doubt was related to his difficult relations with his aristocratic mother, whom he greatly disappointed by not following a career higher than giving parish missions in the hinterlands. His first attempt at starting a seminary was in Vaugirard, but soon, in 1642, the pastor of the parish of Saint-Sulpice in Paris offered Olier his parish in exchange for a benefice Olier owned through his parents' contrivance. Saint Sulpice was the largest parish in Paris, consisting of more than 150,000 people. What Olier created there would be at the center of ecclesiastical life for all of France. The parish did not fall under the jurisdiction of the archbishop of Paris but was independent, which Olier interpreted as an indication that God was calling him to train priests not just for a single diocese but for many.

When Olier arrived at Saint-Sulpice it was among the most neglected of parishes. Olier set to work establishing eight subdivisions, each with a priest in charge. Baptismal and catechetical programs began to take root. The Huguenots and the Jansenists residing within the parish were engaged in dialogue. Within ten years the parish was completely transformed.

Olier's guiding insight was that the way to convert people to the Christian way of life was through good priests. The public worship at Saint-Sulpice was carried out with great decorum. The adoration of the Eucharist was the centerpiece of the parish's devotional life.

In another revelation Olier was told that his tenure as pastor would last no more than a decade. In 1652 he experienced the first of a series of strokes that left him paralyzed. Olier ceded the direction of the parish to others, and during the remaining four years of his life he concentrated his thought upon the development of the seminary, his main work. The rule of life that he formulated for the seminary was designed to implement two purposes: to be a house of studies and to be a place of spiritual formation. He drew inspiration from the teachings of the church councils, the Fathers, and the model of Charles, but really his rule was only a sketch to be filled in by others.

As a house of studies Saint-Sulpice offered courses for everyone in philosophy, theology, morals, and apologetics. The more talented seminarians aiming for academic degrees were allowed to go every day for class at the Sorbonne. Courses in liturgical celebration and pastoral practice were offered within the seminary itself.

As a place of spiritual formation, the unique feature of Saint-Sulpice was the requirement that faculty and seminarians share the same life of prayer, study, apostolic works, and recreation. All were expected to pursue the same goal: to live to the highest degree possible for God and for Jesus Christ. The dynamic of this formation was quite different from that in a seminary of St. Charles.

After completing their training at Saint-Sulpice, the seminarians once ordained spent the next two or three years in community among the priests serving the parish. Here they would apply all that they had learned. By the time of Père Louis Tronson, the third superior general of the society, there were as many as ninety priests in residence.

Before his death at the age of forty-nine, Olier fulfilled his dream of sending missionaries to Montreal to found a Christian outpost in the New World. He dreamt also of sending priests to other French colonies such as Vietnam. The spirituality of the French School was beginning to spread to the entire Christian world.

The Priestly Spirituality of Saint-Sulpice

The work of Jean-Jacques Olier that had the greatest influence on the spiritual formation of priests down to the Second Vatican Council was his *Traité des saints orders*. Published in 1676 eighteen years after his death, it has been translated and republished many times in subsequent years. The volume's editor was the third superior general of the Sulpicians, Louis Tronson. The complete text has been reexamined by a group of Sulpician scholars who published a new edition in 1984. Placed side by side in this new critical edition are portions that can be authenticated as written by Olier himself with Tronson's additions. It is now evident how much Tronson altered both the substance and the style of what Olier had dictated to a secretary after he had suffered a series of debilitating strokes.

Olier's doctrine is centered upon the paschal mystery and our participation in it through the sacrament of baptism. The tone is mystical. In the subtle changes of Tronson, there is another accent, one more clerical and ascetical.[29] In keeping with these different emphases the seminary would become more like a religious novitiate, a place separate from the world where clerical identity could be reinforced.

It was Tronson who oversaw the development of the Sulpicians' first constitution and created the rules to guide Sulpician seminaries. His work, *Examens particuliers*, was required reading for all seminarians. What Tronson had in mind in his publication of the *Traité des saints ordres* was to popularize through his omissions and choppings the thought of Olier. He intended a kind of spiritual directory for the use of seminarians. He gave Olier's thought a different style, making it more literary and toning down its mystical imagery.

The *Traité* made more than stylistic changes upon Olier's spirituality. Tronson's version accents the ascetical over the mystical, the human effort required more than grace. While Olier stressed the balance between the apostolic and pastoral dimensions of the priesthood, Tronson emphasized the clerical. Olier's great intuition, vindicated by Vatican II, was that the whole missionary life of the church is a true living sacrament of the universal salvation offered by Christ; with Tronson, the priesthood alone bears that sacramentality. Olier stressed the essential link between the perfection required of clerics and the holiness to which all the baptized are called.

The overall result was a dangerous rupture between the religious and apostolic dimensions of the priesthood. And because Tronson saw too many careerists seeking the episcopate and mercenary persons accumulating benefices, he downplayed bishops and the unity of bishops and priests. The *Traité* became an expression of a world-rejecting spirituality. Tronson's change of perspective would heavily burden the whole subsequent Sulpician tradition.

First Assessment

In subsequent years various tensions latent in this approach to formation of priests would emerge. I mention three: the human versus the divine, the diocese versus the seminary, the pastoral versus the clerical.

First, the human versus the divine. In the sixth chapter of St. Paul's Letter to the Romans, two moments of Christian existence are set forth: death to self, life unto God. Jean-Jacques Olier went to new lengths in emphasizing the contrast between these two moments. For him, the creature by itself is a nothing coming from nothing, and returning to its own nothingness. The Christian is caught between two extremes, *néant* and *grandeur*. These two polar opposites drive Olier's teaching. For human nature Olier has nothing but contempt. He writes, "The entire mass of the flesh of Adam's children and all its substance is corrupt. Man is depraved to his foundations; he is nothing but an inclination to evil and sin. We are not only sinners, but sin itself."[30]

Only by the most extreme mortification can there be victory in the violent war between the flesh and the spirit. Christ provides the model. "The holy humanity of our Lord," says Olier, describing the Incarnation, "is annihilated as a separate person: it has no interests of its own and cannot act by itself. The person of the Word with regard to itself looks for and seeks in everything only the interests of the Father. Thus is it also with the true Christian."[31]

Second, the diocese versus the seminary. The aim of Cardinal Bérulle was to give to diocesan priests the stature and perfection of life previously the domain of the religious orders. To achieve this goal the seminary must become a "formative community" whose key relationship was that of the priest-mentor to the seminarian. This primary and confidential relationship similar to that of the priest-penitent relationship in confession was to continue into the years after ordination. The seminary faculty alone, not the bishop, was equipped to determine the worthiness of candidates for ordination. The diocese itself was peripheral to the formation process. Since the parish of Saint-Sulpice was not under the jurisdiction of the archbishop of Paris from the beginning, the seminary of Saint-Sulpice was not an integral part of the archdiocese.

This fault line emerged very clearly in 1970 when the bishops of the United States set into place its new Program of Priestly Formation. Conflicts arose since according to Sulpician statutes the seminary faculty, not the bishops, possesses policy-making authority.

Third, the pastoral versus the clerical. The seminaries of the French School emerged from an intense religious culture. Priests were conceived as an elite, separated from ordinary life in the world. The cultic role of the priest was all-important, with the expense of separating the priest from the people. The seminary itself resembled a religious novitiate. The pastoral dimension of priesthood suffered in such a formation. This fault-line was exposed in the failed priest-worker experiment in France after the World War II. Realizing that average workers might never enter a church or meet a priest, priests began taking secular jobs to bridge the gap.

Sometimes this tension is described in terms of a monastic versus a pastoral training, but the issue is more complex. It has to do with the nature of the priesthood itself and differing conceptions of it. As Yves Congar argued in *A Gospel Priesthood*, the priest must be one who is "in front of the people" he is called to serve.[32]

The church of Saint-Sulpice in Paris is remarkable in size, rival-ing even the cathedral of Notre-Dame. Its interior is adorned with the stunning murals of Eugene Delacroix. But the furnishing that best demonstrates the spiritual élan of the French School is the pulpit built in 1789 by Charles de Wailly. It is astonishing. The preacher is placed high above the congregation on a platform accessible by two staircases on either end. According to the critic John Russell, the pulpit "seems to hoist the preacher high above our terrestrial concerns on a flying carpet of marble."[33] The French School thus artistically portrayed provides all the thrills and all the hazards of a magic carpet ride.

Three

The Call of the
Second Vatican Council
A Priestly Formation More Rooted
in the Church Community
and Its Mission to the World

*Through the priesthood which arises from the depths of the inef-
fable mystery of God, that is, from the love of the Father, the
grace of Jesus Christ and the Holy Spirit's gift of unity, the priest
sacramentally enters into communion with the bishop and with
other priests in order to serve the people of God who are the
church and to draw all mankind to Christ. . . .*

— JOHN PAUL II[34]

Nearly twenty years after the conclusion of the Second Vatican
Council, Cardinal Gabriel Marie Garrone, once prefect of the
Congregation for Catholic Education and active council participant, directly addressed what he regarded as a false notion that
had emerged about the council, namely, that it said significant
things about bishops and laity but nothing new about priests. He
stated:

For one who lived through the council, the opposite is the
case. What the council, and specifically *Lumen Gentium*,
reveals is that the priesthood of the ordained is given greater

clarity through its relationship with the priesthood of the bishop. If we return to that source once again, new insights may be provided to priests as well as spiritual encouragement. This labor remains almost totally ahead of us. . . . In the eyes of many, the document on the priesthood itself, falsely once again, seems to have nothing new to say, repeating simply with particular vigor what has been said for centuries regarding priests, particularly by the French School.[35]

Already in 1971, barely six years after the council's close, the international synod of bishops returned to the subject of the ministerial priesthood. The document that it produced noted the concerns that continued after the council about the priesthood — that it was out of touch with the actual world, that priestly identity was still trying to situate itself within a church of many ministries — ministries, with the council's encouragement, now being performed by lay people. As a beginning step to reexamine these pressing issues, the synod underscored what it called the "essentially communitarian" nature of the priesthood and its necessary relationship with the bishop, other priests, and the people. It gave the example of the formation of small communities of priests and people within a diocese as a new means to live out these relationships and accomplish better the mission of the church in the world. Much later, in 1990, another synod would return to the project of priestly formation in the circumstances of today. Its deliberations and conclusions would result in an apostolic exhortation of Pope John Paul II, *Pastores Dabo Vobis* of 1992. That document distilled the experience since the council and set a course for the future of formation.

In this chapter I examine the teaching of the Second Vatican Council on the ministerial priesthood and the formation required for its exercise. I then summarize the important ideas contained in

Pastores Dabo Vobis. In the two concluding sections of this chapter I outline the emerging spirituality of the ministerial priesthood with its new emphases and then provide a first assessment.

The Second Vatican Council's Teachings on the Priesthood

Cardinal Garrone properly stressed that we must look to two great constitutions of the Second Vatican Council, *Lumen Gentium* and *Gaudium et Spes*, the church in itself and the church in the world, more than to the two decrees specifically dealing with the ministerial priesthood and its formation, to understand and appreciate what was innovative and significant in its teaching on the priesthood. It is commonly observed that the decrees on priests, *Presbyterorum Ordinis*, and the decree on priestly formation, *Optatam Totius*, were hastily composed from outlines developed late in the council as it was approaching its conclusion. This latter decree, however, does contain some new notions regarding seminary programs.

Optatam Totius has seven major sections. The first encourages each nation to develop its own program of priestly formation based upon the principles outlined in this decree. This is in keeping with the collegial nature of the episcopate defined by *Lumen Gentium.*

The second section addresses the fostering of vocations. This task is said to belong to the entire Christian community. Minor seminaries, where these still exist, are mentioned as having a role to play. Here and elsewhere in the document the utility of a sound psychological evaluation is noted as a basis for the evaluation of the maturity of candidates.

Major seminaries are the topic of the third section. What is new here is that the spiritual, intellectual, and disciplinary aspects of formation should all be subsumed under a pastoral focus. Bishops, for this reason, should be actively involved in seminary formation; the seminarians should know the bishop as a true father. The seminary itself should be perceived as "the heart of the diocese."

The fourth section, on spiritual formation, once again emphasizes the need for integration of the spirituality being instilled with the doctrinal and pastoral aspects of seminary life. Such spiritual training is not to be a mere exercise of pious practices and devotions, according to the decree, but should be connected with the life of the diocese and its presbyterate. In this section two new notions are introduced that will bear fruit in subsequent years — the idea of a "suitable interval of time for a more intensive spiritual preparation" by the candidates as they more fully discern their calling and the advisability of "some interruption" of studies to do pastoral work. This latter notion of more extended pastoral experience is developed further in the sixth section.[36]

The fifth and seventh sections concern academic aspects of formation. Once again the overarching notion is the need for integration. All areas of study, both in philosophy and theology, should be taught under the general conception of how these fit within the mystery of salvation.

Optatam Totius, as we have noted, is grounded in the ecclesiology of *Lumen Gentium* and *Gaudium et Spes*. Cardinal Garrone and others have pointed out three new notes about the church that are central to these constitutions: the church as communion, the church as people of God, and the church in service to the kingdom of God.

According to Vatican II, the church in its deepest reality is a mystical communion grounded within the Trinitarian life of God that manifests itself in the communal life of the faithful. In the past the church found its analogues within worldly realities such as the civil state. The church like the state was a "perfect society" on a par with, or superior to, other earthly powers. Bishops in this

conception were a kind of royalty and priests part of an aristoc-
racy set above the people. "The Second Vatican Council reversed
this perspective," Cardinal Garrone explains. "It gave priority to
the church's mystery, that is to say, its unique and transcendent
aspect situated in the great mystery of the divine and of the Trinity
itself."[37]

Second, the council wished to place the church within, not
above, human history and asserted that it has a role to play in
history's unfolding. A historical perspective was seen as needed to
offset the Platonizing tendencies that have manifested themselves
over the centuries. The biblical phrase that was chosen to express
this was "the people of God." Within the people of God there
are different roles that complement one another. In the words of
Lumen Gentium:

> Though they differ from one another in essence and not
> only in degree, the common priesthood of the faithful and
> the ministerial or hierarchical priesthood are nonetheless
> interrelated. Each of them in its own special way is a partici-
> pation in the one priesthood of Christ. The ministerial priest,
> by the sacred power he enjoys, molds and rules the priestly
> people. Acting in the person of Christ, he brings about the
> Eucharistic sacrifice, and offers it to God in the name of all
> the people. For their part, the faithful join in the offering of
> the Eucharist by virtue of their royal priesthood. They like-
> wise exercise that priesthood by receiving the sacraments, by
> prayer and thanksgiving, by the witness of a holy life, and
> by self-denial and active charity.[38]

Third, the council strove to orient the church and its mission
toward the coming kingdom of God on earth. The mission of
the church is to announce the kingdom's arrival and to prepare
for God's reign, that new order of things that will bring peace,

justice, and love. Having such a mission, the church must join forces with all persons of good will, learning from them as well as teaching them.

As the constitution on the church flows in an organic manner from a description of the mystery that is the church in chapter 1 to the definition of the church as the people of God in chapter 2 and then continues with a whole new teaching on the role of the laity in chapter 4, some have objected that chapter 3, with its treatment of the hierarchical nature of the church, is a discordant inter-ruption and not consistent with the rest. What the council was doing, actually, was integrating the episcopal and priestly offices within the mission of the church itself. The offices of bishops, priests, and deacons are defined not as dignities but as a service; they are in "service of communion."[39] The spirituality embodied in this theology regards priesthood not only in a vertical relation with God but firmly situated upon earth among the people.

The council for the first time defined that episcopal conse-cration confers the fullness of the sacrament of orders.[40] Priests are referred to as "cooperators with the episcopal order" and its "aids and instruments" in the service of the people of God.[41] Bish-ops participate in an order in the church that is of its nature "collegial,"[42] — that is to say, their responsibilities extend beyond their particular dioceses and parishes to the whole church. Bishops and priests therefore make up one priesthood but with differing functions.

> Associated with their bishop in a spirit of trust and gen-erosity, priests make him present in a certain sense in the individual local congregations of the faithful, and take upon themselves, as far as they are able, his duties and concerns, discharging them with daily care. As they sanctify and gov-ern under the bishop's authority that part of the Lord's flock

entrusted to them, they make the universal Church visible in their own locality and lend powerful assistance to the up-building of the whole body of Christ. Intent always upon the welfare of God's children, they must strive to lend their effort to the pastoral work of the whole diocese, and even of the entire church.[43]

While the council developed its teaching in strict continuity with the teachings of previous councils, especially the Council of Trent and the First Vatican Council, it did introduce these new emphases, which together constituted a somewhat different shape of the priesthood and its spiritual foundations.

Pastores Dabo Vobis

In 1970, the Congregation for Catholic Education issued a new "Plan for Priestly Formation" (*Ratio Fundamentalis Institutionis Sacerdotalis*). While it did not offer any new theological insights about seminaries, it did stress three points: that there should be a return to what the Council of Trent taught about local bishops taking more responsibility for the direction of seminaries, that, while Rome should continue to have general oversight, there could be room for local adaptation, and that, as the Second Vatican Council taught in *Gaudium et Spes*, seminaries should strive to overcome their isolation and enter into greater contact with the world the priests were being trained to serve. With the *Ratio Fundamentalis* as guide, many national programs of priestly formation were developed and revised along these lines over the years that followed. Papal visitations of seminaries took place with the intent of maintaining a strict distinction between the training of persons to be ordained for the ministerial priesthood and that given to laity who were to undertake various other ministries within the church.

Pastores Dabo Vobis is the latest magisterial teaching about seminary formation. As we noted in the introduction, the moment was right for a new comprehensive treatment of the subject since the questions that arose after the council about priestly identity had become less preoccupying. As a post-synodal document it is the distillation of several weeks of discussions by the bishops and therefore somewhat diffuse in its ideas and proposals. It is composed of six chapters.

The first chapter is a survey of the historical situation in which the church finds itself as it addresses the whole area of priestly formation. Under the many "challenges" listed are the obvious ones of growing secularization and weakening church affiliation, especially in the Western world.

The nature and mission of the ministerial priesthood are outlined in the second chapter, drawing upon the ecclesiology of *Lumen Gentium* and other Vatican II documents. The priesthood of the ordained is described as fundamentally relational, situated within the church's deepest identity of being both a communion and a mission. The full exposition of the content of the third chapter, which is devoted to priestly spirituality, will be given below.

In the fourth chapter the vocation of the priest is treated. It is described as both uniquely personal, a divine gift to an individual, and as profoundly ecclesial in nature. All church members without exception are said to have the responsibility of cultivating priestly vocations. Among these the bishop has the first responsibility, along with the presbyterate. Parish communities and individual families also share in this essential task.

The key portion of *Pastores Dabo Vobis* is the fifth chapter, devoted to the formation process itself: its four major areas, its seminary setting, and its agents. The context of this entire setting is contained in this citation from *Optatam Totius*:

Spiritual formation . . . should be conducted in such a way that the students may learn to live in intimate and unceasing union with God the Father through his Son Jesus Christ, in the Holy Spirit. Those who are to take on the likeness of Christ the priest by sacred ordination should form the habit of drawing close to him as friends in every detail of their lives. They should live his paschal mystery in such a way that they will know how to initiate into it the people committed to their charge. They should be taught to seek Christ in the faithful meditation on the word of God and in active participation in the sacred mysteries of the church, especially the Eucharist and the divine office, to seek him in the bishop by whom they are sent and in the people to whom they are sent, especially the poor, little children, the weak, sinners, and unbelievers. With the confidence of sons they should love and reverence the most blessed Virgin Mary.[44]

The specific contribution of *Pastores Dabo Vobis* to the rethinking of priestly formation is its delineation of what it called its four "areas." These areas of formation can only flourish, it declares, if seminaries are considered more than just a "place" but as a spiritual "accompanying" of candidates in an environment in which personal bonds can be fostered with those directing the formation and among the candidates themselves. These four areas are human, spiritual, intellectual, and pastoral.

Regarding human formation, the exhortation stresses character strengths, the ability to relate to others, the capacity for living a life of celibacy, moral conscience, and human maturity that are required of someone able to undertake the heavy responsibility of pastoral ministry and serve as model of the Christian life for others. It notes as being especially important "the capacity to relate to others. This is truly fundamental for a person who is called to be responsible for a community and to be a 'man of communion.' "[45]

Spiritual formation is described as the work of the Holy Spirit and as engaging the entire person. What the Holy Spirit accomplishes in the process of spiritual formation is unity with and conformity to Jesus Christ the redeemer. Following the teaching contained in *Optatam Totius,* spiritual formation is said to have a "triple path": faithful meditation on the word of God, active participation in the church's holy mysteries, and the service of charity to the "little ones."[46] The document underscores the development of the capacity to live a selfless life on behalf of others as critical to spiritual formation.

> Formation which aims at giving oneself generously and freely, which is something helped also by the communal structure which preparation to the priesthood normally takes, is a necessary condition for one who is called to be a manifestation and image of the good shepherd, who gives life (Jn 10:11, 15). From this point of view, spiritual formation has and should develop its own inherent pastoral and charitable dimension, and can profitably make use of a proper devotion to the sacred heart of Jesus.[47]

In the intellectual formation dimension, stress is placed both upon strict standards regarding philosophy and theology requirements while at the same time integrating them with the overall formation and giving them a spiritual and pastoral orientation.

With regard to pastoral formation, pastoral effectiveness in the care of souls is underscored as the overall goal of all four dimensions. The document calls for the development of a true theological discipline of pastoral or practical theology carried out with a plan of progressive experiences. Through these experiences seminarians will learn how to work successfully with other priests already engaged in pastoral work. The parish is the privileged place for such interaction to occur. The seminarians should also be engaged during their seminary years in specialized ministries that serve the poor and promote justice. In all these ways a true grounding will be given of their understanding of the church as "communion."

> Awareness of the Church as "communion" will prepare the candidate for the priesthood to carry out his pastoral work with a community spirit, in heartfelt cooperation with different members of the Church: priests and bishop, diocesan and religious priests, priests and lay people. Such a cooperation presupposes a knowledge and appreciation of different gifts and charisms, of the diverse vocations and responsibilities which the Spirit offers and entrusts to the members of Christ's body. It demands a living and precise consciousness of one's own identity in the Church and of the identity of others. It demands mutual trust, patience, gentleness and the capacity for understanding and expectation. It finds its roots above all in a love for the Church that is deeper than love for self and the group or groups one may belong to. It is particularly important to prepare future priests for cooperation with the laity.[48]

The institution of the major seminary is reaffirmed as the best place for formation to take place, but the agents of formation within the seminary community are expanded to include lay faithful, both women and men, and most prominently the bishop himself, for whom the formation of future priests is a grave responsibility.

On the question of minor seminaries for adolescents, some such community is seen as having continuing utility in the nurturing of potential vocations to the priesthood. Where it is not possible to maintain the institution of a minor seminary, associations and groups can be formed to receive guidance and direction. Older candidates also would benefit from such associations.

Given the growing diversity of seminary candidates and their backgrounds, the document calls upon the Congregation for Catholic Education to gather information about experiments to provide more adequate preparation of these candidates before they enter the seminary. A "propaedeutic period" is mentioned as a possible approach, with its length, place, shape, and curriculum still to be worked out.

The sixth and concluding chapter of *Pastores Dabo Vobis* addresses the continuing formation that should take place without interruption after a priest has been ordained. The entire local church should be involved in a process that encompasses all four areas of formation. Priests should be encouraged where it is pastorally advisable to share a common life. Membership in priestly associations within the diocese can help to create strong bonds with the bishop and the entire diocesan family.

Priestly Spirituality according to *Pastores Dabo Vobis*

Gustave Thils was a major contributor to the drafting of the Second Vatican Council's decree on the priesthood, *Presbyterorum Ordinis*. In 1948 he had written a book, revised in 1961 just before the council opened, on the diocesan priesthood, *Nature et spiritualité du clergé diocesain*. In it he identified "pastoral charity," a newly named virtue, as the "predominate" virtue for the diocesan priest.[49]

In his work Thils drew heavily upon Ignatian spirituality, defining the diocesan priest as a "contemplative in action." He rejected the term "secular" as the identifying adjective for priests not members of religious orders because it seemed to imply inferiority to those priests living the monastic life shaped by vows to live the evangelical counsels. Somewhat defensively Thils writes,

> We are in the world, we must be there, and we want to remain there. But we are not of the world. We are not "worldly." The term "secular" seems at times to insinuate that we are. This regrettable comparison harms, first of all, the priests, whose apostolic mission radically separates them from the world, in life as well as in spirit. It also harms the faithful, who thereby acquire an imprecise idea of the ideals which animate our clergy.[50]

Like the Second Vatican Council itself, Thils used the methodology of *resourcement* to clarify and renew ancient church institutions such as the ministerial priesthood. In his survey of ancient sources Thils was struck by how the scriptures themselves and the early church fathers described the presbyter or overseer-bishop primarily as the pastor of the local church. In his role as father of the flock entrusted to his care, the pastor immerses himself in all kinds of matters requiring spiritual or temporal charity. Thils cites an early pontifical for the ordination of priests that refers in the first instance not to presiding over the Eucharist but to being the bishop's helper, ministers of the second rank, in the exercise of apostolic charity.

Given this background, it is not surprising that *Presbyterorum Ordinis* employs "pastoral charity" as the internal principle guiding and animating the spiritual life of priests. Inasmuch as the priest in his primary relationship is configured to Christ the good shepherd, the pastoral charity of Christ himself must become that of the priest who represents him.

When trying to plumb the depths of the teachings of the Second Vatican Council it is important not only to examine the conciliar documents themselves but also the magisterial teachings that have followed. In this sense the apostolic exhortation *Pastores Dabo Vobis* is of particular significance in elaborating what *Presbyterorum Ordinis* taught regarding priestly spirituality.

Chapter 3 of *Pastores Dabo Vobis,* which takes up the topic of the spiritual life of priests, similarly makes "pastoral charity" its focus. Such charity in the first place requires of the priest the gift of self on behalf of Christ's flock. It has as its source the reception of the sacrament of orders and finds its full expression and most adequate nourishment in the Eucharist. As the council taught,

> This pastoral charity flows mainly from the Eucharisitc Sacrifice, which is thus the center and root of the whole priestly life. The priestly soul strives thereby to apply to itself the action which takes place on the altar of sacrifice.[51]

After discussing the specific holiness to which the priest is called within the universal call of every person to Christian perfection, chapter 3 speaks of the unity of the life of the priest in his spirituality and in his activity in ministry, a unity found in the practice of pastoral charity. As minister of word and sacrament and in his role of presiding within the Christian community, the priest finds his personal path to holiness.

The chapter continues by linking pastoral charity with the practice of the evangelical counsels and of celibacy in particular as expressions of the specific service the priest provides to the people. In the concluding sections, in addition to discussing the call to priests to renew in themselves the grace of ordination, the document underscores how priestly spirituality is grounded in the priest's relationships with the bishop, his fellow priests, and the entire community. It states,

The priest needs to be aware that his "being in a particular Church" constitutes by its very nature a significant element in his living a Christian spirituality. In this sense, the priest finds precisely in his belonging to and dedication to the particular Church a wealth of meaning, criteria for discernment and action which shape both his pastoral mission and his spiritual life.[52]

First Assessment

Earlier in this chapter we cited the observation of Cardinal Garrone that reflection upon the new insights regarding the priesthood and priestly formation of Vatican II remains almost totally ahead of us. A major example is seminary formation.

The Second Vatican Council — according to Pope John XXIII, who summoned it — was a "pastoral" council, intended to bring the church up to date in relation to a new pastoral situation. Since the council, the seminary system, which predates the council, has been asked to perform new tasks. What is being questioned today is how adaptable that system is to these new challenges regarding the priesthood and priestly formation. Can "tinkering" with the present models accomplish the council's vision? Here are some examples of the questions raised.

Seminaries have introduced pastoral courses and pastoral formation programs, but are these an adequate substitute in a "freestanding" seminary for not being at the center of the life of the diocese from which the candidates come?

Propaedeutic programs to provide basic evangelization of candidates and to make up for their academic deficiencies has been widely introduced, but can such programs actually make Christians in a secularized world?

The seminary still operates within the academic model of an academic year that itself derives from a bygone agricultural society in which children were needed in summer to plant and harvest the crops. Does the Holy Spirit who is the agent of formation operate within such confines?

The high Christology of the French School restored to the priesthood a needed dignity and respect, but does it need to be balanced with a Christology that gives greater place to Christ's messianic role as the humble servant, exemplified in the Letter to the Hebrews, where Christ's unique intercession is grounded in human weakness? (Heb. 5:1).

Continued formation after ordination, again within the Tridentine model, is part of the program of *Pastores Dabo Vobis,* but with no curriculum provided. The agency to provide the continuing formation is once again the seminary even though the priests often live far away from such institutions. The issue of "continued formation" is a critical one when we consider that the greatest numbers of departures from the priesthood occur in the years immediately after ordination. Deprived of the supports once found in the seminary community, the diocesan priest finds himself on his own.

In a hint of potential different models of formation still in their nascent stage, *Pastores Dabo Vobis* takes note of "groups, movements, and associations" inspired in different ways by the Gospel that exist already within traditional seminaries. The document speaks affirmingly of such groups, commenting that they are a "nourishing gift of souls within these institutions.... A priest, therefore, may find within a movement the light and warmth which can enable him to practice fidelity to his bishop and make him readier to fulfill the duties and discipline of the seminary, making his faith more fertile and his faithfulness more joyful."[53] During his pontificate Pope John Paul II was particularly attentive to these new movements and the hope they offer to support clergy as well as laity in increasingly secular society.

We have discovered the spirituality of the Council of Trent well portrayed in the *verismo* of Caravaggio and his school, which had the intention of inspiring ordinary Christians to a life of religious conversion and fervor. We have found the sublime spiritual vision of the French School displayed in the murals Delacroix made for the Church of Saint-Sulpice and its magnificent pulpit. But what art form best exemplifies the era after the Second Vatican Council where faith and culture are no longer so intimate? I suggest Abstract Impressionism.

Robert Motherwell, the great Abstract Impressionist, locates the origins of this style in the feeling modern persons have of being ill at ease in the universe, owing to what he describes as the collapse of religion and of close-knit community.[54] Given this cultural milieu, it was not inappropriate that when the University of St. Thomas in Houston wished to commission the art for its new chapel, it turned to an Abstract Impressionist, Mark Rothko. Rothko felt deeply the dissolving unity of religion, philosophy, and poetry. The traditional iconography could not portray with accuracy our current spiritual striving for a harmonious vision of our existence. He covered the four walls of the chapel with solid blocks of brown and red. The viewer, sitting in the center, observes the changing light on these surfaces as the sun follows its course. In this severe, abstract way, the spirituality of our time is clarified. It is a spiritual condition that calls out for such new religious expressions.

Four

The Seminary of the Neocatechumenal Way
Conversion, Community, Mission

Through the preaching and celebrations made in the initial cate-cheses, the Holy Spirit invites men and women of different age, mentality, culture, and social condition, to begin together an itinerary of conversion, based on the progressive rediscovery of the immense and extraordinary riches and responsibilities of one's own baptism, so as to effect in them a gradual growth and matura-tion in faith and in the Christian life. At the end of the convivence, with those who welcome the call to begin this post-baptismal catechumenate, the neocatechumenal community is formed.

— STATUTE OF THE NEOCATECHUMENAL WAY[55]

Pope John Paul II, like Pope Paul VI, endorsed and supported the Neocatechumenal Way, a new instrument to bring back to the church the many who after baptism live far from its influence. Initially begun to transform parishes, the Neocatechumenal Way has developed in the last forty years into a powerful spiritual influ-ence upon the whole church. Pope John Paul calls the Way a work of the Holy Spirit in our times.

Every time the Holy Spirit germinates in the church impulses for greater faithfulness to the Gospel, there flourish new charisms which manifest these realities and new institutions which put them into practice. It was so after the Council of Trent and after the Second Vatican Council. Among the realities generated by the Spirit in our days figure the Neocatechumenal communities.[56]

According to the definition given to the Way by one of its founders, it is not to be identified as a separate movement within the church. Rather, it is doing something that is basic to Christianity itself, helping individuals who have been baptized at birth actually to experience conversion to Christ and his way of life. In canonical terms, the Way has been described as "a lay association in a general sense."[57]

The current process of secularization has brought many people to abandon the faith and the church. Because of this a new itinerary of Christian formation needs to be opened up. The Neocatechumenal Way does not lay claim to forming a movement in itself, but to helping parishes to open up a way of Christian initiation to baptism, in order to discover what it means to be Christian. It is an instrument, in the parishes, in service of the bishops, to bring back to faith many people who have abandoned it.[58]

Soon after his election as pope, John Paul II invited the founders of the Way to join him for Mass. This was at a time when the Vatican had not yet issued official approval and the Way was being criticized for setting up a separate structure for an elite within the church.

In a conversation after Mass the pope told them that as he prayed the Mass he was thinking of them, and the words came to him: "atheism, baptism, catechumenate." He consciously was altering the usual sequence by placing catechumenate *after* baptism, not *before*. This is the exact inspiration of the Way, that those baptized into the church need to be evangelized and converted.[59]

The specific means by which the Neocatechumenal Way seeks to rebuild the church is through the formation of small communities of faithful within parishes. Although this is a new structure for the local church, the tripod upon which these communities are established is a very ancient one: Word or kerygma (the Greek word for the proclamation of the Gospel to potential new converts), liturgy (from another Greek word for the official, public worship of the church), and community (sometimes referred to as "morality" because it is the community that calls the individual to the Christian way of living).

An Itinerary of Conversion

The founders of the Way, Francisco Arguello, an artist, and Carmen Hernandez, a former religious, met in Madrid, where for their own spiritual reasons they both were living and working among the poor. In their attempt to introduce to existing parishes persons who were living far from the church's life and were ignorant of its teachings, they realized that the parishes themselves had to change. The people they were trying to introduce into the church's life and practice needed to feel welcome and supported. This could only be done through small Christian communities within the parishes that could provide such nurture and encouragement. The archbishop of Madrid was fully behind their efforts, which began in the 1960s. Soon the diocese of Rome entrusted a parish to the care of the Way, and later several others. Rome also was where the first Neocatechumenal seminary was established. There are now fifty-two such seminaries from which over a thousand priests have been ordained. By 2006, there will be four such seminaries in the United States: in the Archdioceses of Newark, Denver, and Washington and in the Diocese of Dallas. Throughout the world these seminaries are called Redemptoris Mater (Arch)diocesan Missionary Seminaries.

Although the overall guidance of the Way throughout the world emanates from the international leadership team living in Rome, Neocatechumenal communities and seminaries are inserted in the local diocesan church and its parishes and are subject to the local bishop. The pastor of the parish where the communities exist is called upon to serve as chaplain for their weekly celebration of Eucharist on Saturday evenings, the midweek Liturgy of the Word, and the monthly daylong retreat. The pastor is assisted by a team of lay catechists trained by the Way. These teams are coordinated by the diocesan Neocatechumenal Center, which is usually supported by a separate foundation established by the bishop.

Because the mission of the Way is worldwide, members are invited to become itinerant catechists to establish communities anywhere in the world where the bishop invites them. The itinerant catechist team is made up of a priest, a married couple, and a single man, or by a priest, single man, and single woman. The model is biblical: Jesus sending forth his disciples on missions "two by two." Even in the seminaries rooms are assigned not just to one person but always to twos. Being part of a team is crucial to this way of life.

The spiritual itinerary followed by members of the Way includes an introduction to community life lasting two months, a precatechumenate in two stages, which usually require two years each, then a post-baptismal catechumenate and the final phase of "enlightenment." It is during the phase of the pre-catechumenate that the members are exposed to biblical themes and to the history of salvation. The aim is not merely information but formation, leading the members to the moment of conversion. That conversion is deepened during the post-baptismal catechumenate with instruction in gospel simplicity, liturgical prayer, and private prayer. In the phase of enlightenment, a solemn renewal of the baptismal promises takes place as the member makes a personal commitment to the new way of Christ outlined in the Sermon on the Mount.

During the second, post-baptismal phase, the members are chosen by vote of the community to become catechists. Those selected are called upon to evangelize and build up new communities, either within their own diocese or in another, perhaps even in a distant land. In this way members lay claim to the Christian vocation to become evangelists, leaving home and family for the sake of the Gospel.

A New Model of Seminary

The promotion of vocations to the priesthood and religious life is considered very important within the small communities. Since the original communities were made up mostly of so-called "pillars of the church" as well as others of a more mature age who wished to deepen their faith, the vocations that surfaced were usually older persons embarking on the priesthood as a second career. Now, as the communities grow to include very mixed populations of elders, younger adults, teenagers, and children, the age of candidates for the priesthood and religious life has been much younger.

During the monthly retreats that are part of the community's life, vocation calls are issued. Those who express interest in pursuing the priesthood or religious life are then invited to participate in the vocational program. Once or twice a month, possible candidates for the priesthood gather at the Redemptoris Mater Seminary and meet with a priest or lay catechist. They are helped to examine their lives in light of the Gospel's challenge and to participate in various activities such as a pilgrimage to a local shrine or a hiking expedition. It is only after being a member of a community for three or four years that an individual may be considered as a candidate recommended for seminary.

Once a year all the candidates proposed by the individual communities, several hundred of them, are invited to a retreat in Rome lasting about a week. During this time they meet other candidates from around the world, fast and pray, and listen to talks given by the members of the international team. Then a selection is made, and those selected are assigned to various seminaries all over the world. Two candidates from the same country are often sent together to a seminary so that they can provide each other mutual support.

Even though the Way proposes names for the rectors of their own seminaries, it is the local bishop who must approve their appointment because the seminaries are considered part of the diocese. Seminarians of the Way reside in their own house but attend the same classes offered to other diocesan candidates in the local theologate. The Way has not hesitated to establish seminaries even where such theologates do not exist provided the bishop invites them; in this case itinerant catechists of the Way are called upon to give the instruction. Thus, for example, in the Archdioceses of Newark and Denver, the seminarians of the Way are studying alongside other diocesan seminarians because each has its own theologate. In Guam, where there is no theologate, the Way has full responsibility to train priests for the diocese.

All these seminaries are international in composition, both of the faculty and of the students. The seminarians are ordained for service to the diocese in which they live exist, but with the local bishop's consent they may be sent by the Way to serve as itinerant catechists establishing Christian communities anywhere. For this reason the seminaries of the Way are designated "missionary."

Presbyterorum Ordinis envisioned the creation of such international missionary seminaries as a way to meet the clergy shortage in certain regions, but also as a new initiative to meet new pastoral needs.

> The presbyters should remember that concern for all the churches falls on them . . . and where it is necessary (because of lack of clergy) not only a functional distribution of presbyters should be facilitated, but also the implementation of special initiatives that will favor particular regions or nations of the whole world. To this end, the creation of international seminaries for the good of the whole church according to norms to be established and respecting the rights of the local ordinary would be useful.[60]

The daily schedule of the seminarians by design is a full one. Everyone is expected to attend together the morning, midday, and evening prayer services, the daily Eucharist, and all meals. Seminarians are assigned to teams to perform the necessary tasks of the community. Even recreation periods include the requirement to be a part of a team. In the course of their seminary studies seminarians are expected to serve two or three years as itinerant missionaries. They work in parishes where they are assigned two by two, experiencing how a parish functions and developing pastoral skills. At their mission posting they are integrated into a team composed of a priest and a family with children. While at the seminary they are members of a small Christian community with whom they meet several times a week and thus form stable relationships.

The Spirituality
of the Neocatechumenal Way

The spiritual energy that drives the Neocatechumenal Way derives from extensive exposure to the Scripture as it is lived out in the lives of the persons who make up the community. The word is learned to be lived, to be "echoed," in their phraseology, in the daily experience of the individual person who is on the road to conversion. Scripture, in other words, is intended to "form" and not just "inform."

The community itself becomes the source of spiritual direction. Unlike other seminaries, there are no spiritual directors as such, only regular confessors to administer the Sacrament of Reconciliation. Individuals are expected to participate in the life of the community by sharing how they are trying to discern God's will and how God's will is impacting their lives. Positive and negative experiences in trying to live the Gospel are openly shared.

This is a spirituality based upon a firm belief in God's providence or special care for each individual. It is Pauline in the conviction that all things work together for the good of those who love God. Often cited is the example of Jesus "taking" the three disciples up the mountain of the Transfiguration. The assumption is that they initially were not willing to go there. Later, Peter was able to exclaim, "Lord it is good for us to be here" (Luke 9:33). This is the challenge for all believers: to come to the realization that God has given them their particular situation in life and it is ultimately good that they are there.

This spirituality is very well exemplified in the weekly celebration of the Liturgy of the Word by the small community outside the seminary to which each seminarian belongs. First of all, this is a liturgy, not just a Bible-sharing exercise. The space in which it takes place is liturgical, adorned with a cross, an icon, and a pulpit. There are four readings: one each from the Pentateuch, the rest of the Old Testament, the New Testament apart from the Gospel and a Gospel. These Scriptures are based upon loose lists of selections circulated from the office of the international team in Rome. Often they revolve around a single biblical image derived from one of the biblical commentaries.

The general approach to Scripture is that the Word has been given to question us and challenge us to know ourselves and where we are at this moment in our lives. The first question in the Book of Genesis that God directs to Adam and Eve is "Where are you?" (Gen. 3:9). In Matthew, Jesus asks, "But who do you say that I am?" (Matt. 16:15). The question Jesus directs to the would-be disciples in John is "What are you looking for?" (John 1:38). Only after we have some idea as to where we are in life, what we are seeking, and in whom we truly believe are we ready for the religious answers that the Scripture can provide.

Both at Mass and at the Liturgy of the Word before the priest or deacon gives the homily, members of the community share their own personal experiences of the Word and their struggles to live it more fully. On the basis of such personal disclosure members of the community know each other very well and can evaluate the suitability and readiness of any of its members for orders.

Art and songs are used to express the different stages of con-version. Many of the songs and much of the are the work of Kiko Arguello. The songs with guitar and organ accompaniment use biblical words to inspire the community in their daily prayers.

In a real sense the community becomes the member's family since many are living far from home. As part of their Christian commitment as itinerant missionaries, members are expected to travel anywhere to establish new communities. A missionary tone pervades the spirituality of the Neocatechumenal Way.

First Assessment

The primary characteristic of a Neocatechumenal Way seminary is that everyone is part of a small Christian community. All go to their community's weekly Eucharistic celebration on Saturday evenings, participate in the midweek Liturgy of the Word, and set aside one Sunday a month for a common retreat. The discernment of a vocation to the priesthood therefore is discernment by the community itself of an individual's calling. Community support both before and after ordination explains the comparatively small numbers who leave the priesthood.

Forming a community of diverse human beings is not easy. Neither is living within one. But the community interaction is considered critical in advancing the conversion of the individual member and growth in the faith. Regarding the monthly retreat the founders write, "On one Sunday every month there is a retreat to give everyone the opportunity to talk freely about their own experience of the Word, to say how much it has influenced their lives: at work, in the family, in sexual matters, in social relationships, in connection with money."[61]

Here we already begin to observe some differences from the typical seminary. The candidate is different first of all. He is not just someone who feels called to the priesthood because he wants "to help people" and "enjoys attending Mass," but a person who has had an experience of conversion. Second, while a typical seminarian subconsciously may be given the impression that to be ordained he should keep as low a profile as possible during his seminary years, adhering to the regulations of the seminary in his public life while keeping his private life to himself, the seminarian who is part of the Way is very well known by the community in all aspects of his life.

In answering the question "What are the Redemptoris Mater seminaries," the founders respond:

Experience has shown that combining of a way of initiation
into the Christian life — the Neocatechumenal Way — with
the formation of a presbyter is a great help for the psychological, affective, and human development of the candidates.
Before being presbyters they are Christians, and in the way
of faith they learn prayer, obedience, the sense of the Cross,
to be in communion, etc. Above all, it is a help in unit-
ing the mission with the parish, since the Neocatechumenal
Way is a time of formation that finishes in the parish with
living, adult, missionary communities united to the parish
priest and the bishop.[62]

There is no "seminary shopping" among these seminarians as is
sometimes the case elsewhere. They are told which seminary they
will attend and in which country. Each candidate must answer for
himself the question, "Are you willing to serve as a priest anywhere
in the world?" If the answer is no, he is told to go home.

Separation from home is also part of the dynamic of formation.
In the typical diocesan seminary, seminarians may return home
every weekend and even sometimes during the week. The radical
choice of the Gospel way of life is enhanced if the seminarian
identifies himself with the new community of persons who have
similar goals.

Team spirit is very much part of this way of life. Everything
is done in teams. All things are held in common. Purchases of
clothing and other personal items must be approved by the community; if there is not enough money at the time, the request
must be delayed. Places in the refectory are assigned. Everyone
must be present for every community exercise. There is, then, no
sense that the seminary is a place merely to become credentialed
to become a private practitioner once the person has received
ordination.

For the Neocatechumenal Way, a seminary is not a conveyor belt with automatic progress toward the goal of ordination. How much time a candidate spends in the seminary depends mostly upon the repentance that leads to conversion of heart. There may be interruptions along the way that can last for several years during which candidates found and guide new Christian communities as members of teams of itinerant catechists.

The general tone of these seminaries is biblical in its intensity and simplicity. Their way of living and praying is profoundly participative without being charismatic or conservative in the usual sense. Acts of charity toward the sick, the poor, and the elderly are expected of members of the community. Because of the amount of personal testimony, Masses and Liturgies of the Word can last over two hours.

Criticisms of the Way are not hard to find. As a new "plant" growing in the church, the way is still not easy to categorize in usual terms. Its structure is loose and somewhat ingrown. Materials are shared casually among the communities, and contacts between them are often random. Seminary staff, for example, may be shared through personal contacts rather than more systematic planning.

Situating the communities and seminaries of the Way within the local dioceses and under the authority of the local bishop has not been without complications. Priests who are ordained are under the bishop's direction but also under the direction of the Way. Charges of elitism and exclusivism are heard when, for example, members of a small Christian community do not join the rest of the parish even for the celebration of Easter. The Vatican Congregation for Worship addressed this concern in a letter sent to the leaders of the Neocatechumenal Way in December 2005. Among other guidelines it instructs the communities to participate in Sunday Mass with the rest of the parish at least once a month.

The traditional distinction between what are called the "external forum," the zone of public disclosure, and the "internal forum," the area of conscience and privacy, is understood somewhat differently in seminaries of the Way. While a seminarian in other seminaries might be tempted "to tell them nothing" that might impede his ordination, seminarians of the Way seem required to say everything about themselves within the community sharing.

Professors at the theological faculties where these seminarians go for instruction alongside other seminarians who are not part of the Way have on occasion commented that the seminarians of the Way are not always comfortable with the free exchange of ideas. Having undergone moral and spiritual conversion does not necessarily open them up to intellectual conversion. Perhaps persons who are so heavily committed to the Christian way of life are reluctant to accept anything that might seem to undermine the security of faith.

The French School arose in part in reaction to the dry, academic theology of the time that seemed so separated from Christian life and experience. The Way describes its own retrieval of Christian fervor in similar terms. For this reason some have characterized it as elitist Christianity, a description that in some ways also holds true for the French School. In their own ways both also paint a dark picture of the prevailing religious practice within Catholicism. For the Way, it is almost as if after the era of the early Christians there was a great Fall that the Way was founded to redeem.

> When the catechumenate disappeared over the following centuries, this synthesis of kerygma–change of life–liturgy was lost. The kerygma as a call to faith that implied a moral decision no longer existed. It was transformed into a "scholastic doctrine." Morality became an "internal

forum" — a private act. The liturgy became the same for all. The Neocatechumenal Way recovers this "period of gestation," this synthesis between kerygma, change of life and liturgy.[63]

Like his predecessor, Pope Benedict XVI has been encouraging the creation of small Christian communities like those of the Way because the faith today is fighting for its life, he believes, within a prevailing secular culture. Speaking to a group of priests, religious, and deacons soon after his election, the pope said:

> The ancient church chose the way of creating alternative living communities, not necessarily with ruptures. I would say therefore that it is important that young people discover the beauty of faith, that it is beautiful to have a direction, that it is beautiful to have God as a friend who can truly tell us the essential things of life.
>
> This intellectual factor must then be accompanied by an emotional and social factor, that is, by socialization in faith, because faith can be fulfilled only if it also has a body, and this involves human beings in their way of life. In the past, therefore, when faith was crucial to community life, teaching catechism, which continues to be important today, would have sufficed.
>
> However, given that social life has drifted away from faith — since all too often even families do not offer a socialization of faith — we must offer ways for a socialization of faith so that faith will form communities, offer vital spaces and convince people through a way of thought, affection, and lively friendship.[64]

Pope Benedict resumed this theme when he traveled to Cologne for his first World Youth Day. He urged the youth:

> Form communities based on faith! In recent decades move-
> ments and communities have come to birth in which the
> power of the Gospel is keenly felt. Seek communion in
> faith.... The spontaneity of new communities is important,
> but it is also important to preserve communion with the pope
> and with the bishops.[65]

Kiko Arguello's art is very evident upon the walls of seminaries
of the Way, and it expresses well in visual form the spirituality
of the Way. Kiko once took inspiration in his art from his fellow
Spaniard Pablo Picasso and is said to have won some acclaim for
his work.

After his conversion, however, the art became what we see
in the seminaries — very representational portrayals of biblical
events in an almost naïve form. As with the art inspired by the
Council of Trent, the aim is not merely aesthetic but evangelical,
an aid to interior conversion of heart.

The Neocatechumenal Way began as a way of catechizing those
"from afar," but it has become a life-long commitment on the
part of its members. Given its very recent origin, the Way is still
unfolding as an inspiring work of the Spirit in our times.

Five

The New Foundation of a
Diocesan Seminary in Paris

Ordination is the sacramental act which transforms the very person of the minister, be he deacon, priest, or bishop. Ordination is more than the mere conferral or sanctioning of the capacity to exercise this or that task. Ordination is to be understood as touching the level of a person's engagement in his baptismal relationship with God. As such ordination makes us face the primary and radical question of the response we make to God's personal appeal. In other times, other vehicles would permit us to respond differently to such a question. As the debates among the bishops who have the ultimate responsibility for the formation of priests, the directions of the Council as well as the messages of the synod of bishops and of the pope all underscore, today's situation requires new responses.
— CARDINAL JEAN-MARIE LUSTIGER[66]

In 1979 the diocese of Paris ordained just two priests. Rapid cultural change in an increasingly secularized milieu combined with what Cardinal Lustiger, the archbishop of Paris, calls the "sociologically unstable role of the diocesan priest"[67] have resulted in fewer and fewer persons considering themselves called by God to the priesthood.

With little or no authentic personal religious experience or instruction, the call to serve God and the church in the priesthood has become rare. Formerly priests were known as pastors of stable parishes for their entire lives; now it is uncertain how they are to function. Reflecting upon such present realities, Cardinal Lustiger raised the question of whether the church might have to get on without a priesthood. Rejecting such a notion as being alien to the very nature of the church, the cardinal searched for a new solution to this dilemma.[68]

Without any precedents and going into unknown territory, the archdiocese of Paris in 1984 inaugurated what was called "a spiritual year" for anyone having a credible indication of being called to the priesthood. It was conceived as an opportunity for individuals who might have such a call but did not desire to enter the seminary right away to set in place some foundations that might help them discern their vocation. The aim of the year was to facilitate the first steps in a spiritual journey that would lead to personal conversion to Christ and the gift of self to his way of living.

The "spiritual year" would be a period of dealing with intangibles such as a proper attitude, an opening of the heart. It would help change some preconceptions about the priesthood, that it was just a job and not a personal call from God. What emerged institutionally became known as La Maison Saint-Augustin. From it came the refounding of the Seminary of Paris.

La Maison Saint-Augustin

In 1995, on the tenth anniversary of the founding of the pioneering "spiritual year" for potential candidates for the priesthood, a colloquium was held to assess this new phenomenon that had already spread to other parts of the world. When the ordinary session of the international synod of bishops met in Rome in 1990 to discuss the specific topic of the formation of priests, the participants were assisted by the experience of new initiatives such as the "spiritual year." The results of their discussion were included in the apostolic exhortation *Pastores Dabo Vobis,* which contains the following relevant paragraph.

> While there is a general conviction about the necessity of such a preparatory period prior to entrance into seminary, opinions diverge about its contents and characteristics. Is its primary goal spiritual formation for the discernment of a vocation or intellectual and cultural? At the same time it must be kept in mind that there are numerous and profound diversities among the different candidates and in the different regions of the world. This suggests that there be a prolonged period of on-going study and experimentation so that it be possible to define in a clearer fashion the elements of such preparation or "propaedeutic period." The length, location, shape, and theme of such a period must be coordinated with the years to follow in seminary formation.[69]

In his opening remarks at the colloquium, Cardinal Lustiger sided firmly with the opinion that the spiritual year should not be a "propaedeutic year," simply filling in the gaps in the educational and religious backgrounds of the candidates. For him, it should be a "year for God upon a path leading to God." He made the following six points.

First, drawing upon vocabulary of Ignatian spirituality, the cardinal characterized the year as a time for discernment by the candidate of God's will for him, allowing him in the end to give himself completely to that elected path. Such questions as Should I enter a seminary? Should I consider instead entering a religious order? Should I think of marriage and a career? must be considered. To be able to answer such questions, the candidate must be assisted during this year to achieve full spiritual freedom.

Second, because this period is intended to be foundational for the development of spirituality specifically for a diocesan priest, there must be some connection with the diocesan church but also a necessary personal separation from all previous experiences. This separation is required for a detaching from oneself in order to be converted to a new way of life. The two elements of the spiritual year that accomplish this detachment are the experience itself and its culminating thirty-day retreat.

Third, the general impression such a year conveys is that in a superficial sense it accomplishes nothing — no course of instruction as such, no advancement in fulfilling requirements for a career. Instead the real work is entirely spiritual. Reading the entire Bible and making personal appropriation of its teachings, what is know as *lectio divina,* is one of the tasks. Engaging fully in the sacramental life, especially the daily celebration of Eucharist, is another. Living daily in a community also requires spiritual maturity. Thus the formal studies that follow the spiritual year will have as their foundation the lived Christian life.

In a fourth point, Cardinal Lustiger distinguishes time spent in the academic study of spirituality and its various schools from an actual first step in living the spirituality of a diocesan priest, which is how he conceives the year. He contrasts the experience of some religious novitiates that are later recalled as a "lost paradise" for those who are living the realities of religious life, with what he conceives the spiritual year to be all about. It is a necessary first step in a trajectory spanning the entire life of the priest. It is the time when there are put into place the essential elements of the specific spirituality of diocesan priests: prayer, asceticism, practice of the moral life, love of neighbor, apostolic zeal, and so forth.

The kind of priest the church needs at this particular moment in her history is raised as a fifth point. The cardinal refers to religious orders whose members are trained for a specific mission, such as to the sick or to youth. The priests we need today are persons capable of adjusting to changing situations in the service of God's people. Living for years in a stable parish community is not the prospect today when no one can forecast how the diocesan church will be reconfigured. To be shaped for this kind of service, the individual must be taught how to practice disinterestedness about his own ambitions and obedience to the actual needs of the church as interpreted by the local bishop. Living the community life during formation is also part of that desert experience which is the spiritual year.

In a final point, the cardinal says that the spiritual year can be a time when the community helps an individual work on those imperfections and personal obstacles that need to be overcome for effective priestly service. During the spiritual year a judgment is to be made about suitability for holy orders. That judgment must go beyond an evaluation of professional aptitude to personal qualities. Otherwise, the cardinal says, the candidate could say, "You are judging my fitness without knowing me. I want to be ordained anyway."[70]

The location selected for the spiritual year proved to be ideal. The sisters of the convent of Saint-Augustin offered their facilities, which were at the center of Paris, near the cathedral of Notre-Dame and the archbishop. Priests, deacons, and laity of the archdiocese feel welcome there, and the candidates have access to nearby hospitals and prisons. The desired balance between separation from previous pursuits and engagement in the ordinary life of the archdiocese could be achieved. In the first year twenty-four candidates were in residence along with three priest-directors, who were assisted by two priests who lived elsewhere.

The Creation of a Diocesan Seminary in Paris

The experiment that began in 1984, a year devoted to the spirituality of the diocesan priest, led quite naturally in 1985 to the establishment of the first seminary for the training of diocesan priests in Paris. The Seminary of Saint-Sulpice was never under the archbishop of Paris but rather under the direction of "experts," whose specific mission was the training of priests. Now the archbishop himself assumed his rightful obligation to oversee the training of his own priests. The form such training took was quite different from that provided by Saint-Sulpice.

The curriculum for the six required years of philosophical and theological courses was determined by the Congregation for Catholic Education in Rome, as for any seminary. But in the newly founded seminary of Paris emphasis fell upon the integration of the pastoral, theological, and spiritual dimensions of these studies based upon the foundations already established in the spiritual year.

Instead of a purely academic approach to theological and even philosophical questions, the seminarians found themselves in a community of believers seeking to give faithful witness to the faith of the church. Actual pastoral issues gave their study new focus and relevancy.

Scripture, its study and its personal application, is to be the center of theological reflection, "the soul of theology" as *Optatam Totius* described it.[71] Some few of the seminarians would be invited to become professors, but all are to approach their studies as believers seeking to help fellow believers achieve the "intelligence of faith" as it relates to human affairs.

The methodology adopted by the Seminary of Paris is that of study seminars with open discussion and debate among students and professors. One seminar has to do with the continuous reading of every book of the Bible. A second has to do with how the Tradition of the church and sacred scripture relate to one another. A third is devoted specifically to Tradition and how the doctrine of the church develops within it. In a fourth seminar theological discernment is given to actual pastoral issues. For those seminarians who show the aptitude, study abroad at other theological institutions is a possibility.

The professors of the seminary ideally are younger priests who have achieved a doctorate and have had the experience of at least three years of pastoral life in a parish. In actuality, the faculty is drawn from diocesan priests, religious men and women, as well as laity. Most have other tasks. The professors are asked to relate their courses to the others being offered and to explore together how these individual courses relate to the mystery of Christ and his divine revelation. This coordinated effort is supplemented by the assistance of tutorials.

One of the characteristics of the seminary is that candidates for the diocesan priesthood take their studies alongside candidates for the permanent deaconate, women and men, religious and lay people. Exposure of the seminarians to other walks of life helps to avoid clericalization in their studies.

Unique features of the Seminary of Paris are its separate houses that comprise an urban campus with its focus on the cathedral. In this way seminary life resembles the ancient cathedral schools out of which seminaries emerged in the first place. During the first two years of formation the seminarians are assigned to parish residences, living with the priests who serve there. In the next four years they are assigned to non-parochial institutions where they are exposed not only to parish life but also the diocese itself, with its service to the poor and other works.

The tradition of a thirty-day retreat each year is continued throughout the years of formation. In addition, each seminarian is expected to spend a month in Israel.

The Seminary of Paris has been granted the status of a pontifical theological institute with the ability to grant graduate degrees. As such, the seminary now offers an alternative in the City of Paris not only to the Seminary of Saint-Sulpice but also to L'Institut Catholique.

The Spirituality That Guides the Seminary of Paris

Much reflection went into the creation of the spiritual year conceived as a foundation for seminary studies and the ordained ministry itself. Two characteristics of this formation are personal conversion and the conversion particular to a person called to be a diocesan priest. Is there spirituality specific to the diocesan priesthood? The founders of the Seminary of Paris believe so. Is, then, the spiritual year akin to the novitiate required of those who are embracing the charism of a religious community? The founders respond with an emphatic "no." They want to distance themselves from the quasi-monastic form with which earlier seminaries were identified and create something new.

The overarching purpose of the spiritual year is nothing less than conversion, the total gift of self to Christ made possible by the hard spiritual work of achieving the freedom of spirit required to make such a fundamental, life-shaping decision.

The synod of 1990 sought to define more clearly what it called "the spiritual life of a priest." In one of his interventions at that synod, Cardinal Lustiger defined the conversion particular to a candidate for the diocesan priesthood. He said it is "the gift of one's life to God and the firm intention [*propositum*, the exact term found in the ordination rite] to offer oneself for the priesthood in the manner of the apostles, participating in the apostolic ministry of the bishop, following Christ to the end, even to the Cross"[72]

The elements of such a conversion include the practice of the evangelical counsels and celibacy. Its deepening and nourishment come from immersion in Scripture, fidelity to prayer, the liturgy of the church, and the common life.

In addition to these, Cardinal Lustiger adds another virtue central for a diocesan priest today: adaptability, the capacity to change with the changing circumstances of ministry. Another term for it is "availability" to the directives of the bishop, who must oversee the pastoral needs of the People of God. Such "disinterestedness" of will on the part of the priest is expressed in the promise of obedience given to the bishop and his successors at ordination.

The location and physical arrangements of the Maison Saint-Augustin and the urban campus that the separate residences of the Seminary of Paris comprise are intended to foster this particular spirituality. From the beginning the seminarians are immersed in the life of the diocese and live a communal life. At every point they are involved in apostolic service and participate in the cathedral liturgies as they pursue their studies.

Collaboration becomes a daily necessity in a smaller residence. Seminarians are responsible for living within a budget and performing all the tasks of maintenance.

In making his case for this new form of seminary formation, Cardinal Lustiger asserts:

With the arrival on the scene of new generations of candidates (older, less secure in Christian practice), the "monastic" model of post-Tridentine seminaries would have to be transformed to the point of no longer being recognizable and losing its effectiveness. Experience shows that it is easy in a large [seminary] community to live an isolated life, escaping any true confrontation. The common life in a more restricted group requires that each person face the truth of his life, his own character, and his capacity to relate to others. The capacity to serve (*serviabilité*) becomes a daily test, sometimes painful and burdensome for certain temperaments or older persons with fixed habits.[73]

First Assessment

It was certainly audacious in the very city of Saint-Sulpice, the premier seminary of France whose influence extends far beyond, to "de-institutionalize" seminary formation and create something new. Some are predicting that this experiment may be passé after the life of its cardinal founder. This seems unlikely since it represents a genuine response to the guidelines for seminary formation provided by the second Vatican Council and *Pastores Dabo Vobis*. As the number of candidates it attracts continues to increase and as other dioceses, such as Versailles in France and Denver in the United States, seek to replicate in some form its program of formation, the Seminary of Paris presents itself now after twenty years of existence as a promising new model of priestly training.[74]

The Seminary of Paris is a response to two huge challenges facing the entire church: the dramatic decline in the number of diocesan priests and the need for a new kind of formation for priesthood adapted to a changed kind of candidate and changing pastoral needs. After many centuries of "freestanding" seminaries, the Seminary of Paris represents a return to the kind of seminary envisioned by the Council of Trent centered around the bishop and his cathedral.

In the 1995 colloquium gathered to assess the first ten years of the existence of the Seminary of Paris, Cardinal Pio Laghi, then prefect of the Vatican's Congregation for Catholic Education, made the following observations. First, he said he preferred the term "period of spiritual formation" to "spiritual year." While *Pastores Dabo Vobis* spoke of the value of a propaedeutic period before formal entrance into a seminary, it left to different parts of the world different ways to put it into practice. The Seminary of Paris avoids using the term "propaedeutic period" in preference for spiritual year, but, the cardinal said, there need to be some propaedeutic elements in it beyond the spiritual. He mentioned specifically the study of philosophy, which is all the more important since the candidates are coming from a very secularized environment.

Cardinal Laghi also made reference to those candidates who have discovered their vocation to the priesthood in a lay religious movement. Are they to sever all ties with such movements upon entering the spiritual period or can they continue their association? To continue the formation begun in the spiritual period Paris was able to found its own seminary. What of those many dioceses that do not have the resources to create a seminary of their own?

By distinguishing between a spiritual period and a year of spirituality Cardinal Laghi was touching on an important question: Can conversion of life be achieved within a single year? The answer given by the founders of the Seminary of Paris is that the spiritual year is merely the first step of a long trajectory through the other years of seminary formation and into the priesthood itself.

The Neocatechumenal Way provides some partial answers to the other questions Cardinal Laghi is asking. In their seminaries members of the Way continue in their small Christian communities while studying side by side with diocesan seminarians. Through their network of itinerant catechists dispersed throughout the world, even small and remote dioceses such as Guam can have their own local seminary and program of formation.

The Cathedral of Notre-Dame is located in Ile de la Cité, the heart of the city of Paris and the headquarters of France. Within its few acres were located church, monarchy, and the law. The art critic John Russell declares that Notre-Dame was more than a church and more than a collection of distinguished churchmen — it was the world itself. Its glory now is faded after the Revolution pillaged it, considering it an unwelcome reminder of another, less enlightened age. And yet, Russell concludes, "Nothing can take away the fact that it is essentially a family church, with all of France as its family."[75] By creating his new seminary at Notre-Dame, Cardinal Lustiger was striving to create a new and vital connection between the cathedral and the city.

Six

Implications

This final chapter is called "Implications" rather than "Conclusions" because even though the Second Vatican Council drew to a close forty years ago the proper shape of formation of future priests is still in the experimental stage.

In the chart on the following page various spiritualities and conceptions of the priesthood as well as the values and institutional arrangements that express them are summarized in a few phrases. A common thread through them all is a high estimation of the ordained priesthood. Even in this age when the common priesthood of all the baptized has been rediscovered and demonstrated in the lay ministries and movements that continue to multiply, the ministry of the ordained is regarded as the formative one for the whole Christian community. By common consent, the ordained priest in all his humanity is called to be nothing less than *forma facta gregis ex anima,* the shaping influence on the whole flock of Christ from his entire heart, the one whom the church calls upon to act in the person of Christ in the Eucharistic assembly. The Council of Trent and even Pope John XXIII when he called into being the Second Vatican Council assumed that true reform of the church could be accomplished only from the top down, from the priesthood of the ordained to the lives of people in the congregation. The vibrant and proliferating lay movements and small Christian communities which the Holy Spirit is inspiring today demonstrate that reform can also come from the bottom up,

COMPARISON OF THE FIVE MODELS
OF SEMINARY FORMATION

	Spirituality	Concept of Priesthood	Primary Values	Institutional Model
Council of Trent	Ascetical imitation of Christ the eternal high priest.	Dispenser of the mysteries of God, especially the Eucharist and forgiveness of sin. Soldier of Christ and model to the faithful.	Care of souls. Reform of life and morals.	Military-like training school.
Saint-Sulpice	Divinization of human nature through participation in the life of Jesus, the Incarnation of God.	A spiritual elite. Living representation of Christ the self-giving victim and redeemer.	Self-annihilation. Adoration of God in the Eucharist.	Religious novitiate based upon confessor-penitent relationship.
Vatican II	Insertion in the communion of the church and sharing its mission to the world.	Acts in the person of Christ in offering spiritual sacrifices to the Father. Co-worker with the bishop and servant of God's people.	Pastoral charity. Collaborative service.	To be determined.
Neocatechumenal Way	Personal conversion to the Gospel way of life.	Member of a community. Evangelist and missionary.	Evangelical simplicity. Teamwork. Obedience.	Membership in a formative Christian community. Missionary journeys.
Seminary of Paris	Conversion to Christ in the manner of the apostles and their successors, the bishops.	Servant of the pastoral needs of the local church.	Disposability to changing pastoral needs as articulated by the bishop. Capacity to work with other ministers of the Gospel, lay and ordained.	Spiritual year. Residences located around the cathedral under the guidance of the bishop. Annual thirty-day retreat.

revitalizing the ordained priesthood itself. But no one questions the leadership role of those called and authorized to represent Christ the head among his people.

The various spiritualities and conceptions of priestly life, while they contain different emphases, are more complementary than incompatible. When the first seminaries were created after the Council of Trent, it was believed that the priesthood must be the army of Christ in the world ready and trained to do battle with Satan. That spirituality and that particular form of priestly discipline are being called for again in our day, even in vastly changed sociological and theological circumstances. Jesus appeals to us today as the humble servant who lays down his life for his flock and as the prophet of God's coming reign of peace and love. But at the center of that appeal is the belief that Jesus is the incarnation of the invisible God. Thus his ordained representatives must embrace all aspects, exalted and lowly, in their particular ministry.

Certain elements at the heart of priestly formation, however, are becoming clearer. The experience of a conscious, personal conversion to the Gospel way of life is the necessary starting point of the life-long formation required to equip a priest to accomplish his ministry authentically and successfully. We are witnessing today among younger priests a return to the traditional devotions to the Eucharist, Mary, and the saints, but these devotions alone are not sufficient unless they come from a converted heart. The practice of evangelical poverty and obedience are exterior manifestations of such a heart.

What also is becoming more and more evident is the necessity to reconnect priestly formation and priestly life with the larger community within which the priest serves. The community itself provides realism, nourishment and accountability in the life of the priest. That community can be the local church itself, whose center is the bishop, and it can include as well smaller groupings of the faithful within the local church. The synod of bishops that assembled in Rome in 1987 expressed appreciation that parishes are becoming revitalized in many places when they are reconfigured as communities of many smaller communities that have been formed for mutual support and encouragement in a world increasingly hostile to religious values. Pope John Paul II referred to these newer ecclesial movements and communities in his landmark apostolic exhortation given upon the two thousandth anniversary of the birth of Christ, *Novo Millennio Ineunte.* The pope called them a new springtime of the Holy Church.

Most contemporary seminaries include apostolic works among the requirements for ordination, often to be carried out where the freestanding seminary itself is located, far distant from the candidates' actual diocese. It is becoming more and more obvious that such apostolic experiences are not sufficient. The local bishop, presbyterate, and people all have formative roles to play in the training of a priest.

Yves Congar has accurately observed that when the first seminaries were coming into existence only those supported by a community flourished and survived.[76]

Unlike some dioceses that tried to support seminaries on their own, the Sulpicians, the Vincentians, and the Eudists provided the necessary resources and stability to allow seminaries to thrive. Now, as we know, that is changing. Membership in congregations devoted to priestly formation has declined, and the responsibility of dioceses has become much greater. The liabilities of freestanding seminaries separated from the dioceses are more obvious.

At the Paris colloquium Cardinal Laghi raised the question of whether dioceses with fewer resources than the archdiocese of

Paris could be counted upon to found and support effective seminaries. The pioneering efforts of the itinerant catechists of the Neocatechumenal Way offer some light and some hope in this regard. They have been called upon, for example in Guam, a very remote diocese, to teach basic courses in the diocesan seminary. Sharing resources among dioceses seems less an impossible challenge in the global village. The Neocatechumenal Way and also many religious communities provide the example of their priesthood candidates living in their own houses of formation and taking courses elsewhere.

An active and committed Catholic layman who graduated from the U.S. Military Academy at West Point lamented to me that some priests he knew had shared with him that after seminary they did not feel they possessed the necessary competence and self-assurance to accomplish what they wanted in the priesthood. West Point graduates seemed to him better endowed with the discipline of life and skills required for their profession. What he was pointing out is perhaps a return to the discipline and the élan of Tridentine seminaries, for all their limitations, would be helpful today. I saw some of that firsthand when I visited the Redemptoris Mater Archdiocesan Missionary Seminary in Kearny, New Jersey. The days in the seminary are very structured and very busy. Teamwork in everything is the standard mode of operation. A rigorous simplicity of life was the norm, and obedience to the orders of the superiors to bring the Gospel anyplace in the world was the expectation.

In an insightful article on priestly formation and the new ecclesial movements, Ian Ker, a Newman scholar, makes the point that the program of reform laid out by the Council of Trent would never have gotten off the ground without the aid of the new charism of the Jesuits and Ignatian spirituality. In parallel fashion, he contends, the reform of the Second Vatican Council at this point in history over forty years since the council's conclusion seems to be taking shape through the new charism embodied in movements such as the Neocatechumenal Way.

Just as in the sixteenth century the Jesuits provided a model for the kind of secular priesthood that the Tridentine Church called for, so too in our day the ecclesial movements and communities, by concretely realizing the ecclesiology of Vatican II, are putting before the church a model of Christian communion in which the different parts of the church form an organic and mutually supportive unity. Indeed, to use the pope's own words, they will help to show the rest of the church how "the church itself is a movement."[77]

The greatest implication of this overview of seminary formation is that there is a necessary organic linkage between the seminary and the local church. The good health of both depends on it.

Notes

1. San Carlo Borromeo, *Omelie sull' eucaristia e sul sacerdozio* (Rome: Edizioni Paoline, 1984), 291. Homily given at the ordination of new priests, June 1, 1577; translation by the author.

2. Hubert Jedin, *A History of the Council of Trent, 1545–1547*, vol. 2, trans. Dom Ernest Graf, O.S.B. (London: Nelson, 1957), 356.

3. Louis Ponnelle and Louis Border, *St. Philip Neri and the Roman Society of His Times, 1515–1595* (London: Sheed & Ward, 1932), 192.

4. Concilium Tridentinum, session 23, *De Reformatione*, 18. Translation by the author.

5. Peter Brown, *Augustine of Hippo: A Biography* (Berkeley: University of California Press, 1969), 409.

6. James A. O'Donohoe, *Tridentine Seminary Legislation: Its Sources and Its Formation* (Louvain: Publications Universitaires, 1957), 171.

7. Giuseppi Alberigo, "Carlo Borromeo e il suo modello di vescovo," *Carlo Borromeo e il sio tempo*, Atti del Convegno Internazionale nel IV centenario della morte, Milan, May 21–26, 1984 (Rome: Edizioni di storia e letteraturi, 1986), 206–7. Translation by author.

8. Benjamin Westervelt, *The Borromean Ideal of Preaching: Episcopal Strategies for Reforming Pastoral Preaching in Post-Tridentine Milan, 1564–1631* (Cambridge, MA: Harvard University Press, 1993), 257.

9. Ibid., 271.

10. *San Carlo Borromeo: Catholic Reform and Ecclesiastical Politics in the Second Half of the Sixteenth Century*, ed. John M. Headley and John B. Tomaro (Washington, DC: Folger Books, 1988), 25.

11. Borromeo, *Omelie*, 231.

12. Ibid., 238.

13. Ibid., 142.

14. See *Painters of Reality, The Legacy of Leonardo and Caravaggio in Lombardy*, ed. Andrea Bayer (New Haven, CT: Yale University Press, 2004), 172.

15. Henry Edward Manning, *The Eternal Priesthood* (Baltimore: John Murphy, 1883), 49–50.

16. Ibid., 22.

17. David Lipsky, *Absolutely American: Four Years at West Point* (Boston: Houghton Mifflin, 2003), 10.

18. Ibid., 43.

19. Ibid., 145.

20. Ibid., 106.

21. Ibid., 36.

22. Ibid., xii–xiii, 21.

23. Cardinal Pierre de Bérulle, Narré, appendix to *Discours de l'estat et des grandeurs de Jésus,* cited in *Bérulle and the French School: Selected Writings,* ed. William M. Thompson (Mahwah, NJ: Paulist, 1989), 57.

24. Cited in ibid., 32.

25. Cited in ibid., 11.

26. *Dictionnaire de Théologie Catholique,* vol. 11, part 1, ed. A. Vacant, E. Mangenot, E. Amann (Paris: Librairie Letouzey et Ané, 1931), 1106. Translation is by the author.

27. See Louis Ponnelle and Louis Bordet, *Saint Philippe Néri et la société romaine de son temps* (Paris: Blound & Gay, 1928), 204.

28. Paul Turks, *Philip Néri: The Fire of Joy* (New York: Alba House, 1995), 70.

29. *Traité des saints orders (1676) comparé aux écrits authentiques de Jean-Jaques Olier (+1657),* Edition critique avec introduction et notes par Gilles Chaillot, Paul Cochois, et Irénée Noye, prêtres de Saint Sulpice (Paris: Companie de Saint-Sulpice, 1984), vii, preface.

30. Cited in *Bérulle and the French School,* 43–44.

31. Jean-Jacques Olier, *Pensées choisies,* cited in *Dictionnaire de Théologie Catholique,* XI, 975. Translation is by the author.

32. Yves Congar, O.P., *A Gospel Priesthood,* trans. P J. Hepburne-Scott (New York: Herder and Herder, 1967), 204.

33. John Russell, *Paris* (New York: Harry N. Abrams, 1983), 298.

34. John Paul II, *Pastores Dabo Vobis,* Apostolic Exhortation, *Origins,* April 16, 1992, vol. 21, no. 12.

35. Cardinal G. M. Garrone. *50 ans de vie d'Eglise* (Paris: Desclée, 1983), 25–26. Translation by the author.

36. *Optatam Totius,* Decree on Priestly Formation, *The Documents of Vatican II,* ed. Walter M. Abbott, S.J. (New York: Crossroad, 1989), no. 12.

37. Garrone, *50 ans de vie d'Eglise.* 29.

38. *Lumen Gentium,* no. 10.

39. Ibid., no. 20.

40. Ibid., no. 21.

41. Ibid., no. 28.

42. Ibid., no. 22.

43. Ibid., no. 28.

44. *Optatam Totius,* no. 8.

45. John Paul II, *Pastores Dabo Vobis,* no. 43.

46. Ibid., no. 46.

47. Ibid., no. 49.

48. Ibid., no. 59.

49. Gustave Thils, *The Diocesan Priest* (Notre Dame, IN: Fides, 1964), 265.

50. Ibid., Introduction.

51. *Presbyterorum Ordinis,* no. 14.

52. John Paul II, *Pastores Dabo Vobis,* no. 31.

53. Ibid., no. 68.

54. *The Collected Writings of Robert Motherwell,* ed. Stephie Terenzio (New York: Oxford University Press, 1992), 85.

55. *Statute* of the Neocatechumenal Way, Rome: June 29, 2002, Art. 10, no. 2.

56. Letter of John Paul II approving the Neocatechumenal Way, *The Neocatechumenal Way according to Paul VI and John Paul II* (Middlegreen, U.K.: St. Paul's, 1996), 19.

57. Rose McDermott, S.S.J., "The Neocatechumenal Way: Background, Exposition, and Canonical Analysis of the *Statute,*" *The Jurist* 62 (2002): 96.

58. Kiko Arguello, "Brief Comment for the Vatican Press Office Relating to the Letter of the Holy Father on the Neocatechumenal Way," *The Neocatechumenal Way according to Paul VI,* 21. For an extended exposition of the theology of the way, see Ricardo Blazquez, *Neocatechumenal Communities: A Theological Assessment* (Middlegreen: St. Paul Publications, 1998).

59. Kiko Arguello and Carmen Hernandez, Introduction, *The Neocatechumenal Way according to Paul VI and John Paul II,* 14.

60. *Presbyterorum Ordinis,* no. 10.

61. Kiko Arguello and Carmen Hernandez, "The Neocatechumenal Way: A Brief Synthesis," *The Neocatechumenal Way according to Paul VI and John Paul II,* 133.

62. "The Redemptoris Mater Seminaries," *The Neocatechumenal Way according to Paul VI and John Paul II.* 140.

63. Arguello, "Brief Comment for the Vatican Press Office relating to the Letter of the Holy Father on the Neocatechumenal Way," 21.

64. *Origins* 35, no. 11 (August 18, 2005): 185.

65. *Origins* 35, no. 12 (September 1, 2005): 203. For an assessment of new movements in the church, including the Neocatechumenal Way, see *Movements in the Church: Proceedings of the World Congress of Ecclesial Movements,* Rome, May 27–29, 1998 (Vatican City: Pontifical Council for the Laity, 1999).

66. Cardinal Jean-Marie Lustiger, *La formation spirituelle des prêtres* (Paris: Les Editions du Cerf, 1995), 12.

67. Ibid., 37.

68. Cardinal Jean-Marie Lustiger, *Les prêtres que Dieu donne* (Paris: Desclee de Brouwer, 2000), 9.

69. *Pastores Dabo Vobis,* no. 62.

70. Lustiger, *La formation spirituelle des prêtres,* trans. by the author, 40–41.

71. *Optatam Totius,* no. 24.

72. Lustiger, *La formation spirituelle des prêtres*, trans. by the author, 34.

73. Lustiger, *Les prêtres que Dieu donne*, trans. by the author, 171.

74. Eric Aumonier, "Une formation spirituelle avant l'entrée au séminaire: La maison Saint-Augustin à Paris," *Nouvelle Revue Théologique* 112 (1990): 373–80.

75. John Russell, *Paris* (New York: Abrams, 1983), 246.

76. Congar O.P., *A Gospel Priesthood*, 213.

77. Ian Kerr, "The Priesthood and the New Ecclesial Movements and Communities," *Louvain Studies* 30, nos. 1–2 (Spring–Summer 2005): 134.

Of Related Interest

Christopher Ruddy
THE LOCAL CHURCH
Tillard and the Future of Catholic Ecclesiology

As Christianity becomes increasingly global in its membership and its practices, how will it deal with increasing tensions between the unity of the faith and the diversity of its expressions? How should the papal ministry of unity be exercised, so that, in the words of Pope John Paul II, "while in no way renouncing what is essential to its mission, [it] is nonetheless open to a new situation"? How can the relationships between local churches and the universal church be improved? Building upon the work of leading theologians over the past two centuries, particularly the Dominican ecumenist and papal consultor Jean-Marie Tillard, Christopher Ruddy, whose writings have appeared in *America, Christian Century, Commonweal,* and *Logos,* offers us *The Local Church,* with signposts to guide the Church as it responds to these and other challenges.

Topics include:

Inculturation and evangelization ♦ The quest for Christian unity ♦ The relationship of papal primacy and episcopal collegiality ♦ The ecclesiology of Pope Benedict XVI and its future implications ♦ The centrality of Christology and soteriology to ecclesiology ♦ Baptism and Eucharist ♦ Diverse visions of communion ecclesiology

0-8245-2347-4, $29.95, paperback

crossroad

Of Related Interest

Robert Imbelli, ed.
HANDING ON THE FAITH
The Church's Mission and Challenge

Herder & Herder presents the first volume of the Church in the
21st Century series, sponsored by Boston College. Each volume
brings together the best-known voices in Catholic life and thought,
who meet to discuss today's challenges and tomorrow's hopes for
the Catholic Church in America and worldwide. This first volume
includes original contributions by figures such as Robert P. Imbelli,
Mary Johnson, William D. Dinges, Paul J. Griffiths, Luke Timothy
Johnson, Robert Barron, Robert Louis Wilken, Michael J. Himes,
Christopher and Deborah Ruddy, Terrence W. Tilley, Thomas
Groome, Bishop Blase Cupich, and John C. Cavadini

0-8245-2409-8, $24.95, paper

Please support your local bookstore,
or call 1-800-707-0670 for Customer Service.

For a free catalog, write us at

THE CROSSROAD PUBLISHING COMPANY
16 Penn Plaza, 481 Eighth Avenue
New York, NY 10001

Visit our website at
www.crossroadpublishing.com
All prices subject to change.

crossroad